Animal Magic

Carolyn Press-McKenzie

Animal Magic

My journey to
save thousands
of animals

ALLEN&UNWIN

SYDNEY · MELBOURNE · AUCKLAND · LONDON

First published in 2015

Allen & Unwin
Level 3, 228 Queen Street
Auckland 1010, New Zealand
Phone: (64 9) 377 3800
83 Alexander Street
Crows Nest NSW 2065, Australia
Phone: (61 2) 8425 0100
Email: info@allenandunwin.com
Web: www.allenandunwin.com

A catalogue record for this book is available
from the National Library of New Zealand

ISBN: 978 1 87750 548 5

Internal design by Kate Barraclough
Set in 10/14 pt Galaxie Copernicus by Midland Typesetters, Australia
Printed and bound in Australia by Griffin Press

10 9 8 7 6 5 4 3 2 1

MIX
Paper from
responsible sources
FSC® C009448

The paper in this book is FSC® certified.
FSC® promotes environmentally responsible,
socially beneficial and economically viable
management of the world's forests.

For my mum Judi and my dad Neil, my big brothers Stephen and David and both of their amazing families for years of love and support.

For the HUHA team who are still travelling with me on this magical lifesaving journey.

But, most of all, for my husband Jim and step-children Shaun and Leah who travelled this part of the journey with me.

Contents

Prologue

'ANY ANIMAL GIVEN THE CHANCE IS A REMARKABLE
CREATURE, IF ONLY THAT CHANCE IS GIVEN.'
CAROLYN PRESS-MCKENZIE, FOUNDER, HUHA CHARITABLE TRUST

If I think about it I have always been surrounded by the magic of animals.

Growing up in the idyllic seaside village of Eastbourne our family cat, called Blue Print Press, was the most devoted and constant companion a young girl could ever ask for. Blue arrived in our family several years before I was born. My father had been putting aside some money for new curtains. When the money had been saved, my mother went shopping for curtains, but instead arrived home with a tiny blue point Siamese kitten.

Mum often told the story of why she spent the curtain money on a kitten that day, and in a way it became a family fable. My father had always claimed a strong dislike for cats—he said they were too disloyal and independent—but every Saturday morning my mother would watch Dad sitting on the steps of the front porch, leaning down to slip on his shoes and tie the laces, and every Saturday morning the neighbour's cat would be there ready to assist with my father's routine. After he had tied the laces, the two of them would sit side by side contemplating the day that lay ahead. As my mother watched, my perpetually hard-working father, who during the week left for work as a fruit and vege auctioneer by 4 a.m., seemed to relax and soften, giving the visiting creature some gentle words and strokes, and even a smile. She decided then that it was time for our family, which at that time consisted of Mum, Dad, toddler Stephen and baby David, to expand. It was time to bring the magic of an animal into our home. Knowing my father would stiffen and protest at the idea, she just went ahead and did it anyway, knowing, as she always seemed to, that it was for the absolute best.

As always she was absolutely right.

From the moment I was born Blue was at my side. He had grown into a huge cat with piercing blue eyes and a booming great voice. Any dog brave enough to walk on the footpath outside our home was quickly shown the error of its ways and would know next time to cross the street before passing by Number 9. But to me and my brothers Blue was nothing but gentle, attentive and patient. He wasn't just 'the cat', he was an important member of our family. He drove in the car to the shops with us, he holidayed with us, even on boating trips to the Marlborough Sounds, and of course he always had his own piece of fish on fish and chips Sunday.

When I was old enough to catch the school bus, Blue would walk me to the bus stop and wait until I was safely on board. Then, at 3 p.m. every week day, my mother would smile and laugh as Blue would wake from a deep sleep, stretch and make his way unaccompanied back to the bus stop on the other side of the main road and wait for me to arrive back into his care.

I was thirteen years old when Blue passed away of kidney failure at the age of sixteen. Our whole community mourned the loss of such a local character. Everyone who knew him was devastated, and as for my immediate family, we were inconsolable. Nothing was right without Blue's strong and nurturing presence. But, as always, life goes on and we learnt to cope . . . though we never forgot him.

Eventually we decided it was time to bring another cat into our lives. Beauregard was small and timid; he had come from a breeder who had failed to socialise him and the emotional damage that plagued him in the beginning was severe. But even as a young girl I quickly realised that no matter what the animal's story was, no matter where they came from and what they had been through, it was the here and now that mattered. Each animal that passed through my life growing up had had troubles along the way, but every single one of them learnt very quickly the magic of trust and respect. They learnt that my family treasured them and that they were important, included and safe. And so the timid newcomer thrived and carried on Blue's legacy: being known as exceptional to all who met him.

As a teenager I developed an obsession for horses. Everything in my room was horsey, and horses were the only thing my friends and I talked about. I even had a voluntary job shovelling horse poo, and grooming and driving trotters around the track every Saturday morning. The stables were located at the Hutt Park race course and were leased to several different trainers. My best friend Fiona and I were lucky to work for a trainer who was a kind man, who respected his six or so horses and treated them well. But as I watched the other trainers I learnt my first lesson in fate. The happiness, well-being and safety of these horses all came down to the luck of the draw. As with all animals it was 100 per cent pure fate who their owners were. Being owned by my boss meant good food, enrichment and kindness, but to be owned by one of the other trainers could have meant anything.

The actions of one particular trainer are burned in my mind forever. He had a young horse that wasn't performing well, and as the trainer got stressed about its poor performance, his palpable dissatisfaction caused the horse to become stressed, which in turn caused the trainer to lose his temper and so triggered the horse to act out. Other trainers around the yards would laugh and say we'd best all stay clear when he was having one of his moments. But that day as I was walking around a corner of the stable, square in front of me I saw the two-year-old pacer hog-tied and hoisted upside-down by its legs. The trainer was kicking the horse and cursing at it, calling it a lazy so-and-so and telling it how he'd show it what a loser deserved. The trainer left the horse hanging for another hour or so, then after he had cooled off he untied it and everything was apparently back to normal. Life at the stables carried on.

As a shy young girl, I had not yet found my voice and to this day I regret that I didn't say or do anything. But what has struck me the most, as I look both back and forward, is the effect a human being can have on an animal.

An owner's method of care or treatment of the animals in their charge is their choice, but the effect of poor choice can be devastating or even deadly to an animal. Whether this is brought about by an owner's lack of education, ignorance or just having a bad day, what is most concerning is our culture of turning a blind eye and allowing each animal to just accept its fate.

Animals in New Zealand are big business; racing and farming are both important industries and having animals as pets is woven into the fabric of our society. And yet, if we opened our eyes and saw what is regularly excused within these industries and in many homes, we would be horrified by what is complacently accepted as normal. These 'normal' practices include providing no shelter for livestock; keeping sows in crates and factory farming of pigs; tethering goats on roadsides; chaining up dogs in backyards; cats and dogs being left undesexed to breed indiscriminately; caged birds left with little enrichment; dogs, cats and rabbits being bred in poor and inhumane conditions and very young puppies, kittens and bunnies being taken from their parents for pet store stock.

The *Animal Welfare Act* in New Zealand offers little protection. It is perfectly acceptable to shoot your dog in the head if you feel it is not agreeable to your way of life. It is okay for anyone to breed their pet no matter what their situation is and with no regard for the well-being of the animals or an overwhelmed community. It just goes on and on. Every animal deserves to know the love and safety of a responsible home, whether that is within a business or a suburban backyard, and yet in New Zealand this is sadly often not the case. Surprisingly, safe and sensible homes and businesses are the exception not the rule.

Of course the way forward has to be education. The cycle of suffering at the hands of ignorance and complacency needs to stop.

This book is about the journey that led to HUHA (Helping You Help Animals) Charitable Trust. It tells the story of how I and the amazing team of people I met along the way built what have become New Zealand's leading no-kill animal shelters. I have been careful to leave in my mistakes, as no one is perfect and we all change as we grow. It is my wish that this book not only delights you with the magic of the happy ever afters, but that it also offers penny-dropping moments.

I also want to show you the power of community and of

social media. We are living in an age when anything is possible, especially if we unite with one strong voice.

So, please learn from my experiences, my successes and my mistakes and grow with us. Together we can start to make the changes in our culture that animals so desperately need.

It's true that my cat Blue was exceptional. But that was because he was allowed to be a significant, involved and enriched member of my family. At HUHA we have a saying which we use almost daily as animals with a reputation for being bad, untrainable or useless come into our care.

We simply smile confidently and say, 'Change the environment and you'll change the animal.'

CHAPTER 1

A motley crew

Enter piglet, exit husband.

I'm not sure if it's normal but I didn't cry when my first husband left. Not even a tear. It wasn't that I didn't love him, it's just his leaving somehow made everything seem easier.

We'd only been married for a year and to be fair to Leon the huge changes I was going through had come out of the blue. I was becoming the polar opposite of the tidy, conforming, café-dwelling girl he thought he had married. My father had passed away six weeks after walking me down the aisle. I had announced to the world that I was vegetarian even though previously I had been a voracious steak eater. I had walked out on my apprenticeship as an animal trainer and in the same week I was offered a contract to work as an animal wrangler for a children's television series. And our little first home in suburbia by the sea had unexpectedly turned into a petting zoo, alive with the pitter patter of tiny feet . . . a pig, chooks, cats, a movie-star dog called Bob, nine actor rats and Felix the magpie.

Leon told me the moment of truth was when the magpie I was training, who enjoyed the freedom of our home, backed up to him as he sat relaxed in a bath, shook its tail and plopped a poo into the bathwater.

To be honest, we both realised that the marriage wasn't working and hadn't been the best idea either of us had ever had. After the bath incident, it felt like mere minutes before there was a For Sale sign on the front lawn of our little cottage, a Sold sticker was slapped across it and I was excitedly loading boxes into my very old TK Bedford house bus and heading for 5 acres of ragged swampy paradise on the Kapiti Coast, animals in tow.

Felix oozed personality. He was the first magpie I had raised and if the reports I had heard were true I knew I would be up for at least a year of cheeky fun and entertainment before he would head off to the call of the wild. When Felix was handed to me by my boss, a renowned animal trainer for films and television, the instructions were simple: '*Lord of the Rings* is going to be filmed in New Zealand and if we are to win the animal wrangling contract then we need to start putting the work in now.' My boss had been trying to source some wild rook fledglings from the Hawke's Bay, as they are New Zealand's closest relative to the crows needed for the movie. But as I was just the junior trainer, this fuzzy wide-eyed magpie was to be my practice run at Bird Training 101.

At this time, about eight months before Leon left, my dad, who had been struggling with cancer, was close to passing on. My dad had an amazing skill and uncanny instinct for seeing things for what they were: 'It is what it is, so get on with it'. He had been such an amazing provider for my family. Although he worked all the hours that God gave him, we always had the best holidays together and my memories of growing up in my family are probably the happiest of anyone's I know . . . we were some of the lucky ones.

On the final day of Dad's life I called my boss.

'I am so sorry, I know we have a TV commercial to film, but my father is not going to hold on any longer and I need to be with him,' I said.

She was furious. In her eyes my request was inconvenient and I was being disloyal. She told me that if I wanted a career in film then I had better get my priorities straight. She then said that she was away filming when her father had died and it was that sort of commitment that had gotten her ahead in the business. I apologised profusely and, feeling slightly numb and shaken, went back to my family and my father's side.

I was hand-rearing Felix during Dad's illness, and the little magpie had to go everywhere with me. With all that was going on inside the house, Mum and I parked him up in her glasshouse. It was such a lovely building, housing a grapevine—Dad's pride and joy—that wove its way in and out of the open slats, providing just enough shade so that the sun was not unbearably hot, and just enough warmth to take the bite out of the crisp spring air. Visiting Felix in the glasshouse was cathartic for all of us; he became our little get-away from the reality of what we had to face in the days ahead. As family and friends came to pay their respects and say goodbye, they each in turn visited the glasshouse to escape and to smile, if only for a moment, in the presence of this confident and cheeky little creature.

After Dad passed peacefully, we set about making arrangements for the funeral, with Felix in tow. No one in my family questioned his presence through all the decision-making and organising. He was part of our journey and we were all a little grateful for the light relief. Shoelaces were Felix's specialty. He was usually nestled on my shoulder where he gave me a sense of comfort, but would hop down to floor level and helpfully undo the shoelaces of our visitors, encouraging them to remove their shoes and grieve comfortably. And I allowed myself a smile through the sadness, as my mother, her friends and I numbly wandered through Mum's glorious cottage garden, selecting flowers for the casket. For every perfect flower we lovingly chose and cut, Felix would fly one step ahead of us, snapping away the bees and bugs as though it was his job to usher us through the garden with no interference from nature.

As everyday life carried on I continued to train and care for Felix. Back at our little cottage a few weeks later, Leon and I noticed that Felix was starting to get a head tilt, which worsened over the following day until his head had flipped over his back and was upside-down and looking backward. He was still singing and eating his soggy cat biscuits with great zest but it really did look most alarming and uncomfortable. With our local vet unable to help, we booked an appointment with an avian specialist. He didn't puzzle over Felix's predicament; he knew straight away that I was at fault. I had been killing Felix with kindness.

Cat food is commonly recommended as an acceptable food for rearing young magpies. But being the diligent vet nurse that I also was I had chosen to feed Felix only the best cat food available, staying well clear of the products that were bulked-out with cereal as I thought they were rubbish. But the vet confirmed that it was Felix's expensive dietary habits that were in fact making him sick. As an omnivore his diet should be more varied including the cheap and cheerful brands that were crammed with cereal filler. I had been giving him other food like vegetables and bugs, but with the staple being the posh puss pet tucker, Felix had essentially gone into protein overload. Thank goodness it could be fixed!

Once his diet was corrected, Felix's little head started to

straighten up. And I had learnt a valuable lesson: no matter how much love you give these animals, knowledge of a species' specific needs is vital. I knew I was on a steep learning curve and I couldn't be more excited. I thought about what this funny little bird had meant to my family, and how, in the absolutely worst time in our lives, he had managed to give us the miracle of distraction and humour. I wanted to know everything about these amazing creatures . . . and I wanted to get it right. I decided then and there that ignorance of breed-specific needs was not going to be my style. Knowledge was to be my new bliss.

So just weeks after Leon had made his polite exit, I was living the dream. I was doing well out on my own as an animal trainer, and driving a big and smelly Nissan 4x4 beast. My house bus had scrubbed up nicely, and during the day I could leave the windows open so Felix could come and go—he loved lounging on the couch with the cats in the sun or plucking the petals off whichever fresh-picked flowers I had arranged on the table.

Outside my window, lazing in the breeze, was the most magnificent collection of animals I could ever imagine. At the base of the pile was Drum, a 22-year-old Clydesdale horse, a huge and gentle old man who had come to live with me the day I moved to the country. Under Drum's chin was Dottie, the first pig I had the pleasure of knowing. Between Drum's legs was Mabel the Friesian calf who had come to me at just four days old in a sack. Draped on top of Drum were Ernie and Thistle—an orphaned lamb and a kid goat. And the cherry on the top, of course, was Felix the magpie.

Over the years to come I would befriend a diversity of animals, but the memories of this special bunch will always be closest and dearest to my heart. I treasure the fact that fifteen years later I still have Mabel in my life, but as for the rest of the crew, I grieved for them one by one and said goodbye to each of my special friends as time took them. But I will always be grateful for the life-changing lessons I learnt as I watched the complex relationships form between the different species, as they lived, loved and relied on each other as a family.

When one of them was in a cheeky mood and looking for adventure, I would find myself having to retrieve all of the mismatched crew from whatever trouble they had gotten themselves into. They were never far from one another and it was obvious that they were content and accepting of the traits that each of their vastly differing species brought to the relationship. There was never any doubt that they communicated with one another as I watched, learned and steadfastly cared for and protected them. The detail and skill with which they communicated with me grew too.

Little did I know at the time but this motley crew and the respect and understanding I had for them was to be the beginning of HUHA.

CHAPTER 2

A post-apocalyptic pig

For the next two years I immersed myself in everything animal.

When I had first met Leon I was living on site as a senior surgical veterinary nurse at a clinic in central Wellington. But when our relationship grew, I left my job and my home town to set up a new life with him just an hour's drive away in his home town. Aside from working part-time in a pharmacy I was career-less, and quickly started to feel twitchy. When I heard about a local legend who trained animals for movies I was transfixed with the idea of honing my animal behaviour skills and trying something new.

I approached the trainer about taking me on as an apprentice. There are no special requirements for becoming an animal trainer; you learn on set and by being around it. Of course you have to be naturally good at working with animals, and my problem-solving and veterinary nursing skills helped too. The deal was that for the hours I was learning the trade, I would work for free, but I was also expected to do labouring around the farm, jobs such as thistle-grubbing the 300 or so acres for which I would be paid $7 an hour. My boss decided what was paid work and what was free. She saw it as on-the-job training. So for each long and taxing ten-hour day I would come home with approximately $21 in my pocket. I have never been driven by money, and I saw the value in learning, so I hung in with her for a polite year. But her drive and stony determination meant I couldn't stay a moment longer. Her ethics demanded that I change and toughen, and I didn't want to. I liked who I was.

No one could deny that my ex-boss got very impressive results with her style. I had developed a reputation for being cheerful and easy to work with, and my animals were not as robotic as hers, but that just came down to preference and style; for me, a stress-free environment for everyone, especially the animals, was the key. Within days of leaving my boss, I was approached by a children's television series, asking if I would take the job as head animal wrangler.

The series was about post-apocalyptic child survivors ruling the world . . . but they had a pet pig and a dog and a farm with animals they visited every few episodes to get supplies. In the script the kids formed gangs and ran free, fighting, forming cults and getting pregnant. I'm not sure you could get more far-fetched storylines, but for me the opportunity to live my dream and continue to learn my trade was huge.

For the two years that I worked on the series, I had to have a trained piglet at the ready. The thing is, however, that piglets grow up and so you need to replace them every four or five months with a smaller one. During my apprenticeship I was taught to go to farms to source the animals, to train them, use them and return them. In theory that seemed very practical. But my problem, as it turned out, was returning them. Anyone who has known the love of a pig would completely understand. They are the most amazing animals and are said to be as intelligent as a three-year-old child.

My first visit to a pig farm surprised me because the farmers were scrummy old folk, just like the lovely couple from *Babe*. They smirked and chortled at the idea of one of their pigs becoming a star, and agreed to sell me a piglet that I could return when it had outgrown its role. I sat in their kitchen drinking dark teeth-fuzzing tea with what looked like hunks of clotted cream straight from the udder floating in it. They had a wood burner blazing away with a line of gumboots and socks steaming as they dried. The smell was like nothing I had experienced before. Sweet and putrid would be my best crack at a description.

They owned a small piggery, only 30-odd sows and, as I was about to find out, about 200 piglets. The sows were kept separately in concrete stalls with wooden frames that allowed the piglets to get away from the mother so she couldn't roll on them and kill them. Of course, today I have been to several piggeries, including one that held 10,000 pigs, but this little piggery was my first and the smell and the conditions were something I will never forget. We said hello to the penned mums and looked at their tiny babies suckling away, lying on the sawdust and concrete. They were too small to be trained and on set by the end of the week so we moved on to the large shed.

This old shearing shed was the kind that had a suspended slatted floor. Tap-tapping across the floor with only centimetres between them was a sea of piglets; it seemed like there were hundreds. It was the most crowded dance floor I had ever seen. Apparently these wee fellows were the weaners and this is where they would live until they were ready for eating or breeding. The windows were few and far between, and the smell was intense. I could see the hoses that I assumed blasted the faeces through the cracks of the slatted floor and I wondered how the piglets managed to move out of the way of the freezing water in the winter chill. I suspected they were so jam-packed they couldn't.

So, getting back to business, I decided that these guys and girls were the perfect size to be cast as Porky the post-apocalyptic pig. It was just a matter of choosing one. Oh crikey, how could I choose? I studied them intensely with my casting director hat on and a ponderous gaze. I was really surprised that each piglet looked quite different. The dish of the nose, the flop of the ears, the fear in the eyes . . . they were all completely individual. And yet here they were jammed together, being grown en masse to kill and to eat. No individual needs were being met—these babies had no fun, no freedom, no life. It was clear that they had been fighting, which was not surprising. It reminded me of how my brother David used to thump me on the arm when we three kids were all cramped into the back seat of the family wagon during the long drive to Taupo on our childhood holidays.

But which one should I choose? I cast a look at the section of the shed in front of me, and there she was, her fed-up little eyes looking straight at me. I pointed her out to the farmer who was still chortling at the idea of a movie-star pig and he immediately went into stealth-like ninja mode. Within seconds a surprised little pig was dangling upside down, being held by one leg in a firm farmer's grip. I paid my money and went out the door. I was still a little overwhelmed by everything and was so busy trying to look carefree and chipper that I wasn't really listening to what the farmer was saying to me. But I knew we had agreed that when she was too big for her movie-star role he was happy to take her back. I hopped in the car, popped my seatbelt on, waved a smiley cheery goodbye and as I drove away I knew in my heart that this wee dot of a piglet was never going back . . . not ever.

CHAPTER 3

The best of friends

Collecting animal actors was a learning experience, and I really didn't have a clue what I was doing in the beginning.

Up until then I had been hiring the animals, which involved relying on local owners to be on set on time, or my career would be in shreds. I had formed a wonderful relationship with a local character called Skin. He had the hugest pig that ever walked the earth. She was called Jane and for the random farm scenes Jane and her piglets were just the ticket, rendering the makeshift set with an instantly farm-y look. The downfall of hiring farm animals is that you are never completely connected with them, unless you have the gift of time. Essentially you are just a friendly stranger with lots of nice food. The system works, but it only gets you so far.

So with Dottie safely in my care I set about socialising the nervous little pig. Her time jammed in the barn had reinforced her fight-or-flight instincts, meaning that because she hadn't been able to get away from situations that she didn't like, she would stand her ground and fight. We see this a lot in chained dogs, tethered goats, and penned and caged animals, and to make matters worse for Dottie, she had been taken from the highly charged barn and was now in a world that was beyond her comprehension. Dottie was like a hissy wild kitten, but I knew it was all in the name of self-preservation. My job was to ensure that not only was she safe, but that her life as a free pig was pleasurable and fun. So I stared to detox Dottie from the trauma of her past, the only life she had ever known, teaching her that I was of value to her, which is essentially the key to any connection with an animal. You just work out what they value the most and then become a calm and non-demanding provider. As I worked with Dottie I gave her options; she was allowed to disengage and walk away when she felt unsure, because I wanted her to put that reactive fight trigger right to the back of her mind—and it worked. She started to become more and more precocious and surprisingly confident. As time passed she learnt to seek me out for not only food but tummy tickles and play as well.

Once Dottie showed me that she was beyond simply coping and was now ready to learn, I started teaching her as I would a young puppy by training her to wear a harness, to sit, to stay, to lie down and roll over, to come and to fetch. We never had any bad moments and she soon learnt to trust me. She would storm along beside me around the farm and loved to supervise the other animals. One of her favourite things was to scratch herself against Drum the Clydesdale's legs. Of all the animals Dottie was the bossiest, the princess, the attention seeker. She was always the first to her food and the last one away.

Soon after I had cast Dottie as the inaugural Porky, my next mission was to find an assortment of animals for the farm scenes.

Mabel, the little four-day-old calf, was the most beautiful creature I had ever seen. I had asked at the local food and grain store for where I might find a farmer with some calves to spare. The grain merchant laughed and said at this time of year I could take my pick and gave me the names of some local farmers. When I called one, he confirmed that calves were a dime a dozen that year and the surplus little heifers were being trucked off to the abattoirs with the bobby calves. He agreed to let me come and see his surplus stock with a view to buying one. As I walked into the barn the farmer was busily telling me that he too had an amazing love for animals.

'These girls are my whole life,' he proudly reported, nodding in the direction of about 100 or so cows working their way slowly and surely towards the milking plant.

I watched them ambling along the lime avenue with severely swollen udders, while they called out, belly-rolling bellow after bellow with long strings of saliva ribboning in the breeze from their lips to their shoulders. We were standing approximately 50 metres away in a big open sawdust-strewn barn sectioned off into pens with farm gates. As we walked past the first pen the farmer said the bobbies would be on the truck in the morning. I knew exactly which truck he meant and as l looked down at the perfectly formed little boys, I naively reassured myself that I wasn't part of this horror because I was vegetarian. (Later I opened my eyes and was honest with myself. If you square up and stare down the barrel of reality, the cold hard fact is that society's consumption of milk is the reason that these beautiful creatures die. Seeing the young calves killed because of this social demand is one of the reasons I eventually became vegan. To be honest I am very fit and healthy, and happy drinking my rice milk and eating my soy ice cream, and the best part is that no being has had to suffer or die.)

I met the tiny heifers, some only a day old, in the next pen. The farmer had already chosen the ones that he would raise as replacement milking stock and put them in the end pen, but this group of twenty or so had a less certain fate. The ones he couldn't sell would be joining the bobbies, heading to the abattoir for slaughter.

Why do I always have to pick just one? I agonised as I climbed into the pen.

Their doughy brown eyes were framed by lashes that would be the envy of any woman, and they batted these at me as they surrounded my legs and started to nuzzle and suckle my jeans. I shut my eyes and pointed. As I relaxed my guilt-ridden squint to see which of the dozens of babies I was saving, my heart melted.

She was beautiful. No, she was perfection. I had truly never ever seen any creature so completely perfect.

As the farmer carried her from the barn I noticed a pile of dead calves off to one side.

'Oh no, what happened to them?' I tried to sound cool and unflapped by the distressing sight.

'Oh, you get that,' he said. 'We always lose some, especially in years like this when the milk powder is so expensive. It's just not worth putting the time or money into the weak ones.'

I took a deep breath. 'So does a vet put them to sleep?' I asked.

'No, I just stop feeding them and they fade away. Most of them already have diarrhoea so it's pretty quick and painless. A complete waste, though. I could have sent them to the works too.'

It was more than I could bear. I had no words. I still had no words when he carefully slipped Mabel into a sack and tied the twine around her neck, so, in his words, 'I could travel safely'.

Words still failed me when he gave me his number and said he'd really like to take me out for a nice steak dinner sometime soon. And still no words, just tears, as I drove past the queuing cows, waiting for their breast milk to be pumped into vats, while their vulnerable young perfect babies waited for a truck. But Mabel was safe and now fifteen years later she is still one of the most important friends in my life.

Drum was like a big old oak tree under which both Mabel and Dottie sheltered. And I understood why; he was literally one of the kindest and most steadfast animals I have ever had the pleasure of loving. To tiptoe up and throw my arms around him and then just bury my face in his strong protective neck was my daily indulgence. On my funny little 5-acre block, Drum was like Santa, making every day a lazy dreamy Christmas.

Bringing Drum home had been a spontaneous and unexpected decision, but then so was buying the land and the bus. I had seen an ad for a twelve-year-old Clydesdale, going cheap to a good home, on the grain store noticeboard, and just couldn't shake it from my mind. I was going through so much change, but because of my move to the country and complete independence I was in such a new and liberated state of mind that I thought, Why the hell not! I had always kept horses on leased grazing over the years, mainly wonky damaged ex-racers who I barely rode but doted over and cared for with great diligence—and the thought of actually living with my dream horse was very exciting. So I answered the ad and drove to meet Drum that afternoon.

He was an awesome beast, but with a kind and grand-fatherly way about him. The lady explained that she had driven past him standing alone and starving in a barren stoney paddock in the Wairarapa. After a few more drive-bys, and seeing his state decline, she approached the owner and bought him. It had not taken her long to get the weight on his big bones and the sparkle back in his eye, but due to a change in circumstance she wasn't able to keep him any longer. For me there was never a moment's hesitation. I wasn't convinced that he was only twelve and his back end looked somewhat stiff, but I knew from first glance that it would be an honour to have him in my life.

As I tracked Drum's history it turned out that he was in fact 22 years old, and the stiffness in his hind quarters was derived from a very long and hard career, slogging as a harness horse. His previous owner had driven Drum in a team of up to six, and had used them for ploughing land in early-settler-style re-enactments and demonstrations for a local museum. When Drum's hips had failed and the top vets could not find a suitable solution to keep him in work, he was put out to pasture, except from all reports that pasture was rocky and sparse.

So now this gentle giant was my companion. With supplements in his feed allowing Drum to move freely and without pain, we would amble to the beach together at every opportunity, me astride his broad bare back, enjoying the easy stroll as though I were sitting on a La-Z-Boy rocker. Drum loved the attention and was in his element lounging around with the motley crew, though he was never drawn into their cheeky antics. He was more the anchor, the sensible one. It was almost as if Drum and I were co-parenting.

CHAPTER 4

The magic of breathing

With the addition of an orphaned lamb called Ernie and a young goat I named Thistle, my motley crew for the post-apocalyptic farm was complete.

I would still need to hire in some of the animals for filming, like Jane the pig, but after my experiences with Dottie and Mabel, I made the commitment to rescue, rehabilitate and train any required newcomers. When their roles were over I planned to rehome them into enriching and loving families—aside from the original motley crew who stayed with me for the years to come—and that's just what I did. It was official: I was not going to be exploiting animals for the sake of entertainment, I was going to use the entertainment industry as a vehicle for my rescue work. And, with a few bumps along the way as I learnt my craft, pigs, cows, horses, dogs, cats, rats and others flourished as they left behind the misery of their old lives and embarked on the journey that saw them with a safe and fulfilling future.

I started getting approached about animals in need, and that's how Ernie came into my care. I was back at the pig farm to pick up the latest piglet when the farmer told me they had an orphan lamb and asked if I'd take him. I couldn't resist this vulnerable but strong little soul. As he grew, this little lamb was so sweet and earnest that Ernie proved to be the perfect name. Once castrated and weaned Ernie continued to grow into a surprisingly large sheep, though he remained mild-mannered and gentle. With his diversely enriched and busy upbringing he was never overwhelmed by the crew who offered up an array of cheeky and even bossy personalities. Special Ernie was usually found in the background, quietly assessing each situation, but he never missed out on anything—he was always part of the action.

When I was hiring the goats for the background scenes I decided it would be easier if I trained the goats myself—it would give me a better and stronger connection with the animals as well as an opportunity to diversify my motley crew family. The people I hired the goats from had milking goats and they had a little wether, or castrated, kid that would be of no use to their venture. I named the innocent little creature Thistle and settled him on my sandy and swampy dunes with the others, where he and Ernie became great mates.

As Thistle grew in both stature and confidence I got a lesson in the uncanny ability of goats to get into so much trouble. It was an expensive lesson too. He would squeeze through the seven wire farm fencing, showing young Mabel, Dottie and Ernie the way. On more than one occasion I was called by a politely perturbed neighbour who lived about 600 metres up the road. The motley crew had been a delight to meet, but ransacking the verandah and eating all their pot plants just simply wouldn't do. So I'd dash to the rescue, cheque book in hand, to pay my way out of the awkward situation. And the crew, rather pleased with themselves, would happily trot with me all the way home, promptly fall asleep in a pile and be out for the count while I set about problem-solving the fencing. Thistle was the naughtiness ringleader but I never chained or tethered him; I loved the fact he had the freedom to play with his friends, and to chain him would have just been cruel and lazy. So I battened the fences and as the motley crew matured and grew in size Thistle became somewhat anchored by the others; if they couldn't join him in his mischief he had second thoughts and rallied a game at home instead.

So my little 5-acre block was peppered with just the right number of permanent residents to help me on my mission. Through their confidence and routine the newbies learnt the art of socialising, of trust and respect for all other creatures including humans.

They needed to be a mobile lot, so I bought a home-made tandem walkthrough horse float from an aeroplane pilot for $800. It looked pretty shabby at first glance, but I figured that if a pilot could trust it then so could I. So Drum the Clydesdale, Dottie the piglet, Ernie the lamb, Thistle the kid and a few extras all routinely bundled into the float together, with Drum on one side and the littlies on the other. The nine rats did their acting on the sewer-set days, when the studio was filled with dry ice and steam, and when they were needed they travelled with me in a cage in the car.

Finding the extra animals required for the TV series' constantly shifting storyline was a full-on job as some would be killed off and replacements needed; others, like the piglets, would need refreshing. I would receive the scripts weeks in advance, break them down and then start searching for the 'extras' and training the 'heroes'.

There is a lot of pressure to perform. When I was doing my apprenticeship, I was taught the trade the old-fashioned way: animals worked best when they were starving, not just hungry, but starving. A good two or three days with nothing but a vitamin and mineral supplement paste would do the trick and they wouldn't take their eyes off the prize. If that failed then taking them around the back of the studio, out of sight of actors and crew, and giving them a swift slap across the head meant they wouldn't take their eyes off you. I had learned and listened, I had watched the animals work with the expert precision of a robot. But none of it seemed right to me. Not once did an animal in my care feel hungry or feel the slap of my hand over their head.

In the industry, saying no to a producer or a director is not an option—nor is failing. So I developed my own style very quickly. Trick number one was to always cast an animal that enjoyed the behaviour expected of it. When I was working as an apprentice, I'd go on casting visits, travelling the country for animals with a certain kind of look the director was after. But when I started on my own, my choices were just about personality and a predisposed enjoyment of the behaviour required. For instance, if a dog needed to dig a hole in a scene, I cast a dog that already loved to dig holes, then worked with that behaviour, shaped it and added cues to get it spot on. And of course you had to be sensible; none of the animals could be anxious or shy, and had to be able to enjoy and understand instruction.

Training an animal to work on set involves teaching them body language. I'd always make myself a valued source of what motivated them. I would start with words and conversations, then move to hand signals. That way they learn to defer to you, and not to do anything unless they get a signal from you.

You also train them to work to marks, the positions they need to be in on set, with treats and a clicker. You start with large objects the animal can see easily and send them to stand on or touch the object, and then shrink down the size of a mark to a pebble. The key was teaching the animal confidence at a distance. They needed assurance that just because you weren't at their side, they could still defer to you wherever you may be. And through all of the craziness it always needed to be about focus . . . but the expectations had to be achievable and fun.

Trick number two was to breathe. It's an amazing thing to have such an intense connection with an animal even when you are surrounded by chaos and physically a fair distance apart. The thing with animal actors is that they are just expected to automatically know and understand everything. It's good to get some basic cues set up, but for the most part it comes down to the trainer-animal relationship and the magic link between them when they work. And with Cloudy the standard poodle pup, the newest cast member of the TV series, I had a very strong connection; she watched my every breath.

Cloudy was a replacement for Bob the golden retriever, who the writers had killed off in a malicious poisoning by the baddies. But in reality Bob had just moved to Whitby to live with the series producer and his autistic son. He had been trained to respond to a laser pointer by my predecessor, and with the long days on set he had developed a bit of an obsession with lights and shadows. It became almost like OCD; poor Bob could never turn off. The crew had learnt about his issue and the joke was to flash a light at him whenever they wanted a quick laugh. I was sad to see Bob go. Surprisingly, although my childhood had been blessed with three simultaneous Siamese cats and an assortment of zebra finches and goldfish, and one turtle, Bob was actually the first dog I had ever lived with.

Cloudy was only five months old and full of beans, so for

the action scenes she was stellar, nimble and quick. I would hide up trees, in sewer pipes, in wheelie bins or behind doors. When 'action' was called she would fly with the vigour of a superhero to find me, often pawing at whichever container I was hiding in to show her actor/master where the bad guys had hidden the stash or the baby, or to show the way out of a sticky life-threatening situation just in the nick of time. Cloudy was a great hero. But then came the scenes back at Good Guy HQ, where Cloudy had to sit patiently while the human characters had meetings, stood guard or slept. Asking a five-month-old pup to sit is easy peasy, but asking a five-month-old pup to sit still through seventeen takes of lengthy dialogue is another thing.

To mix things up, on one particular day, the director decided it would be nice for Cloudy to be sitting on the second shelf of a bookcase so she was in full shot.

'Yes, of course we can do that,' I said with great gusto. 'Yes, she will stay perfectly in place through all of the takes you need,' I assured the continuity lady, who also owned dogs and looked a little unconvincingly at my can-do smile.

So action was called and Cloudy sat perched on her shelf. I was positioned behind the camera about 6 metres away. She held her eyeline, meaning she was engaged and focused on me.

'Aaaand, cut. We are going again,' bellowed the director.

Cloudy sat strong through takes one to five, but then her seams started unravelling, she began to fidget and was looking for an out. I had been popping on and off the set between takes to give her a kiss on the forehead and some treats. But the hot lights, the hard shelf and the absolute boredom were wearing her thin.

And that's when the magic of breathing saved my butt and Cloudy's sanity. To connect with your dog by breathing is something that is overlooked in most everyday people–canine relationships and yet it is the most powerful tool. Throughout my 29-year career it is probably the single most important gift I have learnt. I call it a gift because it is truly something special, almost inexplicable. But if I were to try to explain I would say that breathing with your dog is about shutting out the world and simply looking into each other's eyes and truly connecting.

Back on set, it was up to me to steer the ship, and as I calmed my body language and relaxed my shoulders Cloudy started to mirror my actions, matching my slow thoughtful breathing. I shut my eyes as though sleepy, and her eyelids became heavy. No matter what the actors or the crew were doing, no matter how stressed the set around us became, as the scene was repeated time after time after time, Cloudy and I remained in the zone.

'And it's a wrap,' the director finally called with relief in his voice.

One of the assistant directors came over to me and smiled. 'Gosh, Cloudy looks as though she enjoyed just chilling on that shelf. Some days you must find your job is just so easy.'

Soon after starting my contract with the TV series I was called into one of the producers' offices.

'Carolyn, I just thought I'd let you know that I have had a call from a very angry woman.'

My heart sank. What could I have possibly done?

'She claims that you are an impostor and are trying to pass yourself off as her.'

'Oooh,' I said slowly as the penny dropped. It must have been my old boss. Apparently she was mad that I had left her to go out on my own.

The producer, who was a very serious lady and never let her feelings show, gave the tiniest of smiles. 'That will be all,' she said, and I was ushered out of the room.

I guess they knew I was me and that there was no problem . . . but what a funny phone call to receive.

CHAPTER 5

Beethoven and body doubles

I was so excited when I got the job as the animal trainer for a full-length feature film.

The TV series was taking a break and the producer of the feature assured me that filming was only going to be a six-week shoot.

When I received the script I was buzzing and set about breaking it down, working out which animals I would need. The movie was called *Snakeskin* and was essentially about two small-town teenagers so consumed with the desire to have an American-style adventure that they embark on a road trip of the South Island. Along the way they meet all sorts of characters, and end up in a life-threatening chase with some pretty scary skinheads. And that's where I came into it. I was to provide the skinheads' super-aggressive dog. As I read more into the script I found I also had to provide some chooks, some goats and about 60 slimy slithering eels ... easy peasy!

My first call was to my friend Sarah who was working at a local vet's practice. She had mentioned to me that there was a poster on their noticeboard advertising a mastiff cross, an awesome beast in the flesh, and he just happened to be looking for a new home. I called the number and an elderly woman answered and confirmed that her dog Murphy was looking for a new family as he was too strong for her and her husband who both suffered from debilitating arthritis.

Murphy was five years old and had been acquired from a gang headquarters when he was one. Apparently the elderly woman's husband had been working as a case worker and when visiting the address saw Murphy struggling in a cold and harsh environment, so one day he just picked up his chain when no one was home and walked the young and vulnerable pup off the property. But four years later the couple were no longer able to walk Murphy and they had been keeping him at a boarding kennel while they waited for just the right owner to come along.

I decided to check out the 60-kilogram big boy. There was no need to commit, I told myself, it would just be an initial casting interview. As I entered the kennels I was led down a corridor into a small windowless cubicle with four high walls and a small stable door. There was Murphy, a huge bright red monster, in an area not much bigger than him.

'Can I take him for a walk?' I asked the kennel assistant. My instincts were telling me it would not be wise to cramp his style in such a confined space.

The answer was yes and a lead was clipped onto his collar. Well, I am sure if I had been wearing roller skates I could have taken out even the meanest and fastest roller derby team. Murphy pulled with such immense strength along the thin and winding track I literally had to throw my body around a tree and anchor him to a standstill. He was semi-feral from months of being kennelled, and bigger than one of the hounds of the Baskervilles as depicted by Sir Arthur Conan Doyle. But as I zoned into my breathing and he calmed beside me I could see he was really just a big softy, not a scary skinhead dog at all. Nope, he wasn't what was needed for the role and it would be a bad career move to cast him.

As we walked back to the kennel assistant, both of us in a much calmer state than when we had left for our walk, I nodded and said, 'Yes, I'll take him.'

He may not have been right for the movie, but there was no way I was putting him back in the cubicle . . . and, anyway, I was a little bit in love already.

Back at the bus Murphy was amazing, though that first night was a little hairy. Murphy made himself comfortable on the couch, and responded with a low menacing growl if I tried to sit next to him or move him. I knew it was up to me to find a way for us both to process our new relationship. It was my responsibility to be confident and give him direction. His hard edge softened the more he learnt to listen and respect me and as we developed our sensible and safe pecking order, I learnt some things about myself as an animal trainer.

I could teach any animal to do just about anything, but bringing Murphy into my life was different; he wasn't there to learn from me. It seemed that I was there to learn from him. He was my first real-life project. Of course I had been around socially damaged animals before, such as my childhood family cat, Beauregard, some of the race horses I had worked with and even Dottie and Mabel in the beginning. But Murphy was my first canine with real social issues. I had to put the work in and not fail this big boy.

As I started to develop a strategy I thought about how much the wrong environment could damage a life. So, as I taught him to defer to me, and showed him that I was a calm and confident leader, I kept him engaged, enriched and busy. The more he learned and understood our relationship, the more the old inappropriate behaviours faded and the happier Murphy became. As our connection deepened his past life became a distant memory.

Pondering on my not-so-failed failed mission with Murphy, I may have found myself the companion that I never knew I wanted. But I still needed to cast the scary skinhead dog. Then the phone rang. It was Sarah from the vet's again: she had just seen a client who had a Staffy cross called Beethoven, who she described as a 'moving hunk of muscle'.

Beethoven was the real deal. His family lived at Otaki Beach in a converted garage and Beethoven's adoring mum was proud to tell me of his gang connections. In fact, the story was surprisingly similar to Murphy's except Beethoven had been older when he found his freedom. He had been used for breeding and fighting before this gutsy lady had told her family no more and took charge of his destiny. For my purposes he was perfect. I told her that I would need to take him away with me for at least six weeks and I could pay her $600. She agreed with a smile and told me what made him tick, his likes and dislikes. Top of the dislike list was other dogs. Given the opportunity, she said, he'd kill them. So it was decided that Beethoven would be my travelling companion. I was going to train him to growl and bark on cue and I would keep him safe and happy.

I received an odd reaction when we first walked into the makeshift office in Methven, where we were based for the shoot. Beethoven and I had been travelling all night in my 4x4 beast with home-built trailer in tow. We were tired but enthusiastic, and very keen to get the keys to our room. As I sat down at a desk to await further instruction I could hear the production team talking about me—right in front of me as though I wasn't there. As I puzzled at the bizarre conversation unfolding I was suddenly spoken to:

'Yes, you're just the right size, you'll be perfect.'

I looked blank.

'We need a body double for Melanie Lynskey, the lead actress, and you are just the right size!'

They were on a tight budget and as I was only doing the animal work they thought they'd found the ideal solution. 'But we won't pay you any extra, is that clear?'

It was very clear. I wasn't being asked, I was being told.

'Okay,' I said, half-bemused and half-disbelieving. What did I know about acting?

I then found out that I was to share a unit with Helen the production accountant, an absolutely lovely lady whom I knew at once I'd get on famously with. But as I opened the door to our home for the next six weeks there was an immediate and serious problem. There Helen sat reading a book with Freya, a very sweet little fox terrier, perched on her knee. I am probably the least demanding person in the universe, I really don't ask for much, but I had to explain to the admin team that I couldn't be near other dogs because Beethoven had a very real ability to kill them. I really thought I was heard. No, I was told, there was no alternative accommodation available for either me or Helen; we'd just have to learn to manage. So for the next six weeks Beethoven spent his time working, sitting or lounging in the beast or asleep in bed with me . . . and the system worked. Phew.

When you work with animals all day you sometimes forget to think about people and their needs. When I was introduced to the three actors who were playing the skinheads I instantly warmed to them. They were clearly animal lovers, but Charlie Bleakey, the youngest, seemed subdued in Beethoven's presence. With a little prodding I was told that he actually had a very real fear of dogs. Because he and Beethoven were to work together closely it was decided that I needed to spend as much time as I could with the skinhead brothers to dilute Charlie's fears.

What no one warned me about was a thing called method acting. It's when the actor absolutely immerses him- or herself in the character for the duration of the project. There is no off-switch, they are their character 24/7. And that's just the way Oliver Driver, who played Speed, the leader of the skinheads, liked to tune his art. This is great for him and the movie, but as we were spending time together and my mission was to acclimatise Beethoven to the ins and outs of being a skinhead dog, I found my new normal was clutching on to Beet in the tray of the skinheads' ute, being violently hurled around corners with blaring music and a flood of 'Oi's' being shouted from the cab. On one hand, it wasn't exactly easing Beet into the role slowly and carefully, desensitising him to stimuli, on the other we were more than prepared for the high-speed car chases by the time the director called action. Though I must say my thoughts still go out to the gentle community of Methven who also had to endure the method acting on their quiet suburban streets.

Who knew that my role as body double would work so well in my favour? I didn't have an animal-handling assistant so Beethoven's care and safety was all on me. Back home, while filming the TV series or a commercial, I could always call upon my mum to join me on set to help with the A to Bs. This is when you release an animal at mark A with the camera rolling, and the animal then has to land at mark B. As Beethoven was to be involved in high-speed chases, I was worried about who was going to give him treats and reassurance at mark B, which was more than 500 metres up the road. Well, as luck would have it, the lead actress did not have a driver licence so I was thrust into wardrobe and make-up and as action was called, it was me driving the car that the skinheads were chasing with such venom. As we hit the end mark and screeched to a halt, there was Beety excitedly smiling at me Staffy-style when I got out of the car and approached him. Yay for low-budget movies; they are just my thing.

Beethoven was loving all the action and adventure and, actually, so was I. His acting was great . . . maybe there was a little too much smiling in between the growling and barking, and he had a little habit of wrapping his lips around his teeth so it could be argued that his snarling wasn't as full-bodied as I would have liked, but that was being fussy. Beety rode that ute tray like a professional yachtsman as it keeled around corners, his eyeline was good and he was very nice to any fellow actors/victims that the skinheads picked up along the way and threw in the ute tray with him.

I had had my hair dyed and cut to look like Alice, Melanie Lynskey's character, and when Melanie sprained her ankle in real life I was required to be her legs. That meant I was filmed setting a car on fire and pushing the car and a dead body over a cliff. My best work, though, was running in the dark through cattle yards full of stock while been chased by an American cowboy . . . who was also a snake . . . while he was shooting at me/Alice with a pistol.

And then there was the scene where I had to plunge my legs into the foot well of the car, which happened to be full of eels representing snakes. Maybe that doesn't sound so hard, but I was the animal department and so I first had to catch the 60-plus eels, keep them hydrated and safe, execute the scene with movie-star precision and finesse, and then return all 60 eels to the exact position of the river I took them from.

So you're probably wondering how you go about finding 60-plus eels. I had started phoning eel farmers well before leaving Wellington. It took a bit of doing, but I managed to find one up for the challenge, whose nets were about a three-hour drive south of Methven. And that's where the home-made horse float came into it. I had travelled all the way down from Wellington carrying old carpet for the sole purpose of transporting the eels. I had exactly two days to drive south for the eels and be back on set in time to film, then drive the eels home again. All up, that was twelve hours' worth of driving alone.

As I pulled up to the spot on the river I had been directed to, a man in waders approached me. He was laughing to himself.

'Do you think you can do it?' he asked.

I wasn't really sure what he meant. Did I think I could handle the eels, did I think I could keep them safe and alive, did I think I could stick to the timeline? There were lots of questions and the only answer I could give was yes to all the above. I was not in the business of killing innocent eels and I could not be late to set with them either.

He pointed at four large nets bobbing in the debris about 2 metres from the edge of the icy cold river. Oh my, there were so many and they were so big. Thankfully the eels remained in the nets as we laid them across the wet carpet in the back of the horse float.

It's a strange feeling ferrying 60-plus eels behind you; it almost sends shivers up your spine. As I arrived in Methven, it wasn't long before I had to jump into costume, load the eels into the foot well of the car and do several takes of me seated with snake-like eels slithering around my boots. I was then asked to pull my knees up toward my chin, as though in fright, for several takes. Then I put the eels back in the nets and tethered them to a stake in a private stream, which I had prearranged. They were safe overnight and Beethoven and I were up early in the morning to deliver them back to their home as per my promise to the Department of Conservation (DOC) to return them to the specific area they came from. The thinking behind that is to not mess with the eel's gene pool or introduce any new disease. I'm not sure if the eel farmer wanted them to stay in their nets so he could cull them for eating, but I had paid for them fair and square and so I released them with the hope that maybe next time they'd be wiser and steer clear of the net.

Before long the movie wrapped and I was back at my day job on the TV series. I returned Beethoven to his very proud mum and handed over a scrapbook of the work he had accomplished: photos of him acting, photos of him hanging out with Kiwi movie stars and photos of us travelling and our road trip together. I was always so impressed by Beethoven's mum. She was from a different world to me, but the one thing we had in common was a love and an utmost respect for animals and, in particular, the love we shared for one driven bundle of muscle called Beethoven.

Several years later, long after Beethoven would have passed, I sat in disbelief as I watched a news report about a woman who had been murdered by an enraged family member . . . it was Beethoven's mum. I had a little cry and thought that at least they would be together, away from all that's hard in life.

Growing up under the careful watch of Blue, our family cat.

McCavity, a very special cat who arrived as a homeless rescue at Central Wellington Vets and stayed with me as my best friend and companion until he passed away at the age of nineteen.

Although the marriage didn't last, my first wedding was a very special time for my family as Dad passed just weeks later. With Leon and me are (from L to R) my sister-in-law Sarah-Jane, brother David, Dad, Mum, sister-in-law Fiona and brother Stephen.

The house bus, with horses Drum and May.

Some of the motley crew: Thistle, Ernie and a new porky playing with Dottie.

One big blended family.

Training Cloudy for *The Tribe*.

Here's Beethoven, the hunk of scrumminess I trained for the New Zealand award-winning movie *Snakeskin*. He's with Oliver Driver who played the tough skinhead lead.

Dressed up as Melanie Lynskey's body double for the role of Alice in the movie *Snakeskin*.

The Peruvian pinktoe tarantula spider being placed on the actor ready for action in *The Lost World*.

Hand-raised Gerber the parrot swinging on the set of *The Lost World*.

Jim's amazing message to me, carefully spelled out with car tyres, as a surprise on my birthday, two days before our almost-wedding.

Our beautiful wedding day. Here with Leah and Shaun, and Jim's mother 'Grandma Carly'.

Haggis was my wedding bouquet.

At home with Munchkin, Ned, Haggis and Scooter (now rehomed as Cilla).

In a bath of herbs, Orlando the goose with his terrible neck wound. They said it couldn't be healed, but with some HUHA magic and herbal remedies he recovered perfectly within six weeks.

CHAPTER 6

A tired dog is a good dog

Oh God, I was seriously in a pickle.

Cloudy the poodle was due on set in a few hours and she had gone AWOL. She had totally disappeared.

As Cloudy grew into adolescence she had become quite the character. She was just so darn smart. Cloudy actually belonged to the TV show but was able to live with me full-time while I was her trainer; essentially she was the star and I was the hired help. She had a great life on my 5-acre block but the problem was (as with most adolescent dogs) that you really couldn't take your eyes off her for a moment or she would be staring down the barrel of mischief. We had had a few days off between shoots and on that day in particular the callsheet had us scheduled back on set at 1 p.m. I was distracted with office work, and the boredom was starting to get to Cloudy.

My philosophy is 'a tired dog is a good dog' and it's one that I usually so passionately live by. If dogs are kept busy and enriched and they're either mentally and or physically exhausted during the day, then they are not as likely to look for something else, or even something naughty, to do. They are also less likely to develop bad habits such as barking, digging, fence guarding or escaping. To be honest, if a dog is playing up, think about the day you have provided them with and often you've only got yourself to blame.

Cloudy had struck up a firm friendship with Nugget, a slightly older wirehaired pointer I had rescued from a shelter to rehab and rehome. Together, the two of them were double trouble. On her own Cloudy would have got into mischief in full view of me as she liked to stick close and engage in constant conversation. But with Nugget on the scene Cloudy didn't need my reassurance and she had someone else to rely on to take the lead.

That meant that I was now looking at the open gate of the purpose-built deer-fenced dog park that I had left them to play in while I had my morning shower.

Cloudy had opened the latch, which ironically was probably something I had taught her to think through during a TV scene. My block of land had ramshackle farm fencing and beyond it was an abundance of super-fun sandhills. So I jumped in the 4x4 beast and raced the 600 metres or so to the beach. I drove up and down madly calling. If I didn't have her safe and on set for her afternoon scene, I could kiss my job goodbye.

I paced and pondered. I had no doubt she'd be chasing a rabbit somewhere in those dunes, but they stretched for kilometres and unless I could pinpoint her location I had no way of breaking her attention and calling her back.

In between calling out 'Cloudy' and 'Nugget', I dashed onto the bus and rang the studio.

'Hi, it's Carolyn here, are we on time today? . . . We are? Okay, well is Cloudy absolutely necessary in that scene? . . . She is, okay. Cheers, thanks.'

As soon as I put down the receiver the phone started to ring. It was the producer. She could sniff out trouble on the horizon from miles away. I didn't even have a chance to explain. She said that she was expecting Cloudy on set in a few hours—'no excuses'—and hung up.

I paced up and down and called into the dunes some more. If only she'd look up from what she was doing and listen; she had amazing recall.

I just needed to be in earshot . . .

Desperate times called for desperate measures.

I picked up the phone again.

'Hello, is that Kapiti Helicopters? I wonder if I could hire you this morning for a quick job. I've lost two dogs on the sand dunes . . .'

The copter man was so understanding and said he'd call back in half an hour—if the dogs had not returned he would deploy his helicopter . . . and for a very affordable price.

Thirty minutes passed, with no sign of Cloudy or Nugget. I was standing in the galley of the bus with Felix pecking at the toggles on my jumper, totally oblivious to the drama. I felt panicked. Although it wasn't a life-and-death situation, I really prided myself on being reliable. I took my job seriously and I had made a promise to myself very early on that letting down a producer or a director wasn't an option.

I picked up the ringing phone.

'Yes, they are still gone,' I said. 'And allowing travel time to get to the studio, that gives us just one hour to find them.'

I was hanging up the phone when I saw some dune grass rustling in the distance. I ran off the bus so fast I scattered Felix, who gathered himself and flew down to my shoulder. There they were, the terrible twosome, leaping across the dunes towards me, bursting with excitement and as though they couldn't wait to tell me all about their adventures. I threw my arms around the dogs, gave them a drink, cancelled the helicopter, and loaded them and Murphy into the beast. Murphy drove wingman with me into Wellington, while Nugget and Cloudy lay unconscious in the back. There was just enough time for a quick spit and rub with a hanky, like my mum used to do to when we kids were heading off to school. Sand was sprinkling out of Cloudy's dense curly coat as it began to dry, and from close up she looked like a canine pepper shaker.

On set Cloudy settled among the child actors for a long scene . . . thank goodness it wasn't a high action day as she truly was exhausted. Her mood was perfect and as the director thanked us both for some great work, I thought to myself as I smiled, A tired dog is a good dog.

CHAPTER 7

The lost monkey

My next big project was a BBC production, a full-length film adaptation of Sir Arthur Conan Doyle's novel *The Lost World*.

Once again, the timing luckily coincided with a hiatus from the TV show. It would mean six weeks away from my bus and my furry family, and a friend who in the past had enjoyed looking after my life while I was away was not available this time. So I decided to hire a bus sitter. She was perfect, old enough to be responsible, but young enough to have no prior engagements. I showed the sitter how to pump water from the bore and light the Califont for the gas-heated water. She met the motley crew and was introduced to my collection of rescued rats that lived in a two-storey manor under the awning of the bus. Felix seemed at home with her, as did my pet cats, and I had farmed Murphy and Cloudy out to very good friends.

This was a big-budget movie, with the big-budget actors Bob Hoskins, James Fox and Peter Falk—exciting and serious stuff. I read through the script which was about an explorer setting off on an Amazon adventure in search of a lost world of dinosaurs and other extinct creatures. I made a list of the animals that I would need to provide: cart horses, marauding camp dogs and chickens, pigs, a parrot, exotic insects and moths, some eels, a tuatara, a monkey and a tarantula spider.

Straight away I could see that this project was going to be a different kind of challenge. My rescue and rehomed animals were not going to fit the bill so I was going to have to rely on other people. I got to work in the six weeks of preproduction time I had been given. Before the cameras were set to roll, every last detail had to be locked down with precision, with absolutely no room for error.

After a recce of the South Island locations I organised some old-fashioned drays to be transported to a family on the West Coast who had a horse training business and they busily set about teaching some of their horses to pull the carts. I spent a few days in Nelson with a breeder working with her Basenji dogs so they wouldn't react to chickens. Basenjis are hunting dogs, and also one of the most ancient breeds, so while they were the most ideal casting choice with a strong prey drive and an aloof nature, they were a challenge to train. I borrowed some eeling nets and found the best spot for an easy stress-free-as-possible catch and release at a river nearest to the location where the eels would be needed.

I arranged the two-day hire of a monkey and the one-day hire of a tuatara. The tuatara came from Orana Park, the local wildlife park. They knew the movie was coming to town and were really relaxed about hiring out their tuatara as long as it was accompanied by a staff worker. One tuatara in particular had been on educational visits before so he was chosen as the star.

I visited the basement of a university research department where I was shown shelves of click-clack containers each housing a tarantula. I chose the Peruvian pinktoe over the

Chilean rose as I thought its soft pink toes would contrast nicely with the actor's jacket it was to be placed on. I ordered a giant Atlas moth (the world's largest) to be imported in larvae form from Malaysia to a certified butterfly garden for incubation and I hired a capuchin monkey called Tuku Morgan's Underpants, plus his trainer. Last on my list was a parrot that I first met as an egg and then purchased from the parrot ranch just a month later while she was still a fledgling, so I could hand-raise and train her myself.

It was all about timing. It wasn't the finding and coordinating of the animals that was so exhausting, it was more the momentous piles of paperwork and endless ticking off of checklists that came with so many unusual animals and being so reliant on other people. The tuatara needed DOC permits to travel from its home and had to be insured for a million dollars. I had to imagine every worst-case scenario and then show them how I'd manage the risks. The Atlas moth needed consent from both DOC and the Environmental Risk Management Authority and for the monkey I needed to jump through hoops with the Ministry of Agriculture and Fisheries (MAF) to ensure there would be no glitches with either people's safety or the monkey's containment. To give you an idea of the detail, DOC requested that I even pick up the horse poo, so any seeds they might have been eating in their feed wouldn't start growing in the wrong places.

One day before filming I popped into the BBC's preproduction office in Wellington and was called into one of the producers' offices.

'Carolyn, I just thought I'd let you know that I have had a call from a very angry woman.'

My heart sank; this was sounding all too familiar.

'She claims that you are an impostor and are trying to pass yourself off as her.'

'Oooh,' I said slowly as I tried to read the producer's face. She had worked with my old boss before and I didn't know if their relationship was a good one or if she was wise to her pattern of behaviour. This producer was also a very serious, but kind, lady.

She let out an amused laugh. 'All I can say is that I am thrilled it is you who I employed and who is sitting in front of me right now!'

Thank goodness! Sabotage attempt number two failed. Crikey, I was going to have to grow a thick skin to be in this business.

Finally we started filming. I had hired a few locals to assist me, who were family of the horse trainer. They were most definitely interesting characters, not at all what I expected or was used to. Halfway through the project I had already begun to suspect them of stealing from me. Then they conspired to walk out if I didn't up the thousands of dollars that they were already being paid, and the worst part was they would take the horses with them. It was decided between me and the producer that blackmail was not acceptable and we let them walk. Luckily I had a dear friend up my sleeve who had just finished as a Ringwraith in the *Lord of the Rings* trilogy. He was on set and being his usual capable and lovely self within a day. New horses were sourced and we quickly brought them up to speed. Problem solved.

After that most of the shoot went to plan. The Basenjis' performance as marauding camp dogs was marvellous; the hours I had put in the month before had been carefully followed through by the breeder, and the dogs were flawless.

These former bird-killing dogs didn't even look at the chooks pecking around their paws. On the day of his cameo, the tuatara was driven to the location, bodyguard in tow, and insured to the hilt—no different to a Hollywood star. He sat nicely on the rock I had so carefully chilled with an ice pack in an attempt to keep him and his metabolism slow and steady. As an extra precaution, I eyeballed all the producers and told them to lock down the set—we could not afford to lose this guy.

The tarantula arrived in her click-clack container with her guardian from the university and was a great hit among the actors and crew, and little Gerber the parrot, who I named after the pocket knife that all the cool gaffers had on set, was loving all of the interaction and attention behind the scenes.

But overall this big-budget and high-pressure movie did not come without its problems. I remember arriving on set one morning to hear that the prosthetics trailer had caught on fire and a lot of the valuable ape costumes had been destroyed. It was a devastating blow for the film, and the production team quickly went into damage control in a professional and calm manner.

But that was not all they had to deal with. At about the same time, we had gone into the Nile River valley to film a cutaway, a one- to two-second transition shot, of the monkey I had hired . . . and would you believe it, he ran away!

We set up the shot, with Tuku's handler standing by to release him into a tree branch overhanging a creek. I had briefed the crew to be quiet and considerate while the handler communicated with her monkey. I stood back on the bank watching, unable to help as I didn't have a relationship with the gorgeous little creature. And as little Tuku was let go and the filming commenced he chattered and played in the branch as though he had not a care in the world. But when the scene was over and the handler asked Tuku to return to her shoulder, he ignored her. The crew stood by patiently at first and waited for the cue to move on to the next scene. But the monkey remained in the tree, and the director got impatient, calling for the next scene to be shot despite the little primate not yet being secured. I felt helpless as I saw Tuku jump into the boughs of another tree and then out of our sight. The handler and I made a desperate dash to follow, but he was gone.

Oh God, it was my worst nightmare. I was beside myself with guilt, worry and panic. This was definitely a career low. The thing that struck me the most was that I seemed to be the only one who was really and truly rocked by the missing monkey. For the others it was inconvenient and obviously not a desirable outcome but as it didn't slow production, no real harm was done. The joke on set was that they were going to change the name of the movie to *The Lost Monkey*. I wasn't in trouble legally because I had not trained the monkey myself and had no relationship with him. And in the weeks that preceded the filming I had been smart enough to ask the monkey's trainer to sign a waiver assuming all responsibility for the monkey's safety. But morally I felt awful. I was head of the animal department and ultimately I felt the buck did stop with me.

The trainer was quickly given a nice payout for her troubles after she pointed out rather forcefully that when the monkey took for the bushes the crew did not stop rolling, but continued to film the next scene and a rather noisy one at that. And I think she was right; we had a small window to coax Tuku back, but the focused director pushed on without a moment's hesitation. So, cashed up and monkeyless, the trainer headed back home to the little zoo she already had for sale. I couldn't help wondering if releasing a monkey into the stunning wilds of the Nile Valley, although definitely by accident, wasn't a nice resolution to her pending retirement.

It was at least four days before I was needed back on set

and I had stayed up all night writing a long-winded step-by-step account of what led up to the monkey breach for the powers-that-be at MAF. So as soon as the sun started to rise, with the blessing of the producer, I set about hiring a tracker. Jack was the real deal, an amazing cross between an Aussie Outbacker and an authentic Kiwi West Coaster. He had spent years abroad in Australia learning the art of tracking from Aboriginal tribesmen, and he just happened to be in the area and available for hire.

With Gerber settled as usual on my shoulder, I set off with Jack into the bush. Putting aside my anguish and concern for Tuku, I stopped for a moment to take in the environment. It was breathtaking. The bush was so plush; layer upon layer of native vines draped and fell among the tall, strong magnificent trees with dense shrubs and ferns nestled at their feet guiding us along the leaf-littered paths. It was heaven on earth, and I could only hope that Tuku felt the same and that he had adventure not fear on his mind. As we worked our way into the bush the tracker looked at every branch and stone with expert precision. He would stop every once in a while to show me the tricks he'd learnt in the Outback. He'd snap a sweet nut from the centre of a ponga fern to assure me that there would be abundant food here for Tuku, and Gerber would happily accept the find as her own.

Jack was right; there were plenty of nuts and berries, and small animals and insects for Tuku to feed on and I was confident that his natural instincts would have most certainly kicked into action. What did worry me though was the cold; the night air was so crisp and Tuku was used to sharing his bed with the other monkeys at his zoo. As we walked some more the tracker explained that we were getting close to a river and that open beaches of sand can be ideal in showing up telltale footprints. As we reached the clearing I could hardly believe my eyes. There in the soft sand on the banks of the river was a little set of footprints weaving in a zigzag to the water's edge. I just stood there in amazed silence for a while, feeling just a little of the pressure that had built inside me release.

I wondered out loud, 'Why is he zigzagging?'

Jack, who had one knee in the sand by the little prints and his arm resting on the other, turned and looked up at me, his eyes smiling from under his wide-brimmed hat.

'Because he's been playing,' he said simply.

I looked closer at the small tracks in the sand, searching for some sense, and there, intermingling with the first, was a second set of tracks, but these ones were the tiny imprints of a cloven hoof. The tracker nodded as he saw the recognition on my face and in his Aussie-Kiwi twang confirmed my excitement. Tuku had found a kid goat to play with. The monkey had spent a cold night in the wild but he was alive and he had a friend.

After searching the area extensively and not finding any more clues the tracker made his apologies and went back to his business. However, I was determined to cover all the bases. The sound department had done me a huge favour, and while I was in the bush they found the time to drive to the zoo and make a recording of Tuku's monkey troop calling that evening. So with Gerber on my shoulder again and a battery-powered amplifier under one arm and a cat-trap under the other, I headed back into the rain forest to try again.

It was a very surreal experience sitting in the most dense and lush bush, playing with a beautiful little parrot and listening to the haunting call of a monkey troop blasting from an amplifier. I must have sat and waited for hours. In my mind I hadn't quite planned it all out. My mission was clear enough but there were some tricky aspects, such as how I was going to actually convince Tuku to go into the trap and how I was going to keep Gerber from becoming a monkey snack if Tuku did indeed turn up. Well, first things first. Just seeing or hearing him would at least be a good starting point and the rest I was sure I would work out.

Several more hours passed and nothing, just the roaring of cicadas under the rich green light-speckled canopy. I thought it was probably time I should call it a day and be getting back. As I bent to pick up Gerber from a little twig, leaf and apple climbing frame I had built her, I heard a noise behind me. As I spun around in fright I saw a figure appear from the bushes. It was a man. He was just standing and staring, completely transfixed. He didn't look right, in fact he looked disturbingly not normal. I stood rigid, not really knowing what to do. 'Hello,' I said, going with the if-in-doubt-be-polite philosophy that my mum had taught me. He didn't respond, just continued to stare. I could feel myself starting to panic; I was deep in the bush, literally no one for miles and this man was really starting to seem more than a little sinister. My mind was racing through several scenarios when I was suddenly jolted back into the present.

'Carolyn, how are you getting on?' a voice boomed from the other side of me.

The scary man turned in one swift movement and was gone, while out of the shadows stepped the tracker.

'I was a little worried about you out here all alone, so I just thought I'd check in.'

I seriously have never been so relieved to see a familiar face in all my life.

It turned out the man in the bush was familiar to the locals. He was mentally disabled and would often wander off on his own. Although he was known to act oddly he had never harmed anyone. I turned down the tracker's offer to take me to dinner as I got the feeling that wives were hard to come by in his part of town. And as kind and helpful as he was, that was taking my gratitude a little too far.

To this day I am still devastated that I couldn't find Tuku.

But despite the opinions of many who say he would have died from the cold, I remember the bounty of the bush, the food and the companionship available to Tuku and I still hold out hope that he had his happy ever after, living the life of a wild animal without the confines of a chainlink enclosure, just the way a monkey is meant to.

Back at the bus, things had not quite gone to plan. My sitter had broken up with the boyfriend I never knew she had, and had bailed on her agreement to stay and care for my animals after just the first week. Despite my checking in with my mum and best friend Vicky the vet while I was on the road, they had never let on that between them they were taking turns at feeding and caring for my crew. And when I returned it was clear that they had done such a selfless and amazing job.

Unfortunately at that time Leroy Brown, one of the rats, disappeared. I looked for him high and low but to no avail, and I accepted with remorse the fact that as so much time had passed he would be long gone.

A few weeks after I had arrived back from my travels I needed to get something out of the old dark and dirty shed that I had stacked with the bits and pieces that didn't fit in my bus. As I pulled up the rickety roller door, what transpired was like a scene from a horror movie. I casually stood in the doorway of the shed with the sun on my back, allowing my eyes time to adjust to the darkness. Suddenly a small object came flying towards me, projectiling at a rate of knots. As it hit my chest I braced myself, waiting for the pain that I thought was inevitable. But instead the object scurried up onto my shoulder and burrowed into my hair. I was on the verge of screaming and launching into a full-blown arm-flapping fit, when I suddenly realised who my attacker was. It was Leroy Brown the rat, who had somehow found his way into the shed. He was in absolute raptures to see me. It was such an unbelievable moment. A little one-year-old rat who I had rescued as a youngster had such a strong connection with me that even after seven weeks living it hard he knew my voice, my shape and my form. He knew he was safe in my hair and it would seem he had desperately missed me. Once again I was speechless and bewildered. I knew my feelings for Leroy were strong. But until that moment I had never truly understood what an amazing, loving, intelligent and completely underestimated creature a rat is.

CHAPTER 8

Jim, and a new home

I was loving life. I worked hard and, although I have never been a drinker or done drugs, I played hard, mostly dancing all night with my single friends.

But my married friends, who barely ever saw me any more, were starting to worry that I was turning into one of those self-important stuck-up movie types, spoilt and self-indulgent. Thinking they had the right single man to save me from myself they introduced me to Jim.

Our first date went okay. Jim was nice enough but it was really clear to me that he was still rocked after his first and only love, his schoolteacher wife, had run off with a parent of a student just a year earlier. She initially left him in sole charge of their two-year-old and six-year-old but they were now working with a week on, week off custody arrangement.

On the second date he was bringing his kids to visit the animals and have lunch on my bus. Leah was cute as a button.

The forthright three-year-old strode straight up to me in her shiny new red gumboots and in a big booming voice asked, 'What's for me?' Slightly taken aback I offered her the bunch of flowers sitting on my kitchen bench and she nodded with approval. Seven-year-old Shaun seemed less demanding, but he transfixed me with his laid-back cheeky smile the moment he leapt up the clunky big steps. I had never entertained a man and his young children before and I really wasn't sure what would be considered cool.

There was an air of desperation about Jim, not desperate as in wanting to impress me, but more like he was desperate to make his family whole, or happy, or maybe both. So I decided to put my own terror and inexperience with children to one side and try even harder to give them a special day. The naughtiness in me wanted to give Shaun and Leah a special memory with Dad that their mum couldn't beat. Jim looked like he needed a win.

So I went to my bench and placed a box down in front of the kids.

'This just arrived in the mail. It has come special delivery for my work,' I said.

They looked puzzled as I carefully opened the box and lifted out a Chinese takeaway container.

'Can you guess what's in here?'

Leah and Shaun shook their heads with anticipation— they could tell it was going to be something good. Their eyes widened when I explained to them that I needed this special item for a scene we were filming the next day, but then I would have to post the package straight back to scientists in Auckland so the special item could go back to its family in a laboratory.

I slowly lifted the lid and inside was the hugest Avondale spider you could ever imagine.

'Woooooow' was the reaction from Shaun, Leah wiggled with squeals of horror and delight, and Jim just looked happy.

We all took turns holding the spider carefully and I told them how you can't really train a spider like an animal, but there are ways you can manoeuvre them during a scene. For instance, by gently blowing through a straw from behind them you can get them to walk forward and by smearing Vaseline across an actor's arm, a barrier they won't cross over, you can get them to stop where you want.

The spider was a hit and the gorgeous little family seemed to forget their troubles for a while. We went outside to groom the motley crew and have pony rides on Drum, the world's biggest horse. Then we sat down to lunch, chatted and laughed. We talked about what the kids loved to do and how much they loved their Grandma Carly. But there was still a sadness bearing down on them. It seemed to me there was a piece missing and I wasn't sure I was ready or even the one to fill the gap. I gave them all a hug and waved them on their way.

My parting words to Jim were: 'Go and experience life, have some fun, then call me.'

One morning Felix didn't fly down to help me with my chores; he just sat on a branch of the biggest macrocapa tree and watched me. He also didn't come to bed that night. I could hear his cheeky song and could sense that he was happy, so I decided not to panic, just to breathe and wait and see if my special boy was finally submitting to the call of the wild. I had had Felix in my life for more than the expected year and had been bracing myself for this up-and-coming reality, as by nature's clock it would surely soon be time for him to fly the coop. Other magpies had started to visit and swoop around the property, and while there was never any animosity between them and Felix, he had always remained close at my side and watched them with wide eyes.

I woke the next morning to the comforting sound of Felix's song. But immediately I realised he wasn't alone; another playful tune intertwined with his, and then another and another. As I slid open the loft window in my old TK Bedford bus and looked up into the bows of the big macrocapa there they were, six glorious magpies speckling the branches. And to the left of them singing his heart away was my special little Felix, all grown up and ready for new adventures. I climbed down the loft ladder and ran outside.

'I love you little buddy, please stay safe, and please visit me as often as you can.'

I knew he understood, as he always understood. This remarkable creature had made such a huge impact on my life. But to see him with his own kind just seemed so right and so natural. My job was done.

Felix did bring his family back to visit, but as time went on the visits became less and less. I'd gaze at them in the trees and whisper, 'Fly, be free little man.'

Now that Felix had found his family . . . maybe it was time that I extended mine?

It was almost exactly one year later that I had a call from Jim. He was passing through my town and asked if I would mind him stopping by.

I didn't even recognise him at first; he was tall, confident and much more dashing than I remembered. We started looking for a home together just a month later. It needed to be close to the kids' school and with enough acreage for the motley crew . . . and whoever or whatever came next.

A listing in the private sales section of the real estate advertisements caught my eye.

'Character villa with horse arena and round pen on 13 acres. Offers from $165–$195K would be considered.'

Oh, that was cheap, and it was in the Hutt Valley, just 30 minutes from the kids' school. As we drove up the long gravel driveway to the funny old villa perched on a hill, we reserved our judgement and just took it all in. The house was essentially a shell that had been burnt out in an arson attack before being relocated to the property for renovation some day, although it appeared that day had not yet come. It needed a huge amount of work but at least it had a nice new roof.

The land consisted of three hills and three gullies facing north for premium gorse-growing ability. But the potential was there and the elevated views of the valley, a mixture of farmland and native bush with even a distant snowcapped mountain, were to die for. As Jim and I walked the boundary we stopped to admire the horse arena and round pen; we never imagined that we could possibly own anything as fancy as an arena, but it would be so handy for my movie work. When we took a closer look, we saw that the arena was essentially a 40-by30-metre area where the fertile top soil had been removed and sold, and then the exposed bare clay just sprinkled lightly with woodchips and edged with old tyres. Jim sighed and leaned against a round pen post which in turn wobbled and leaned against me.

Among all the gorse and ragwort, which in themselves would be a lifetime mission to clear, this odd little property felt right—and it also felt affordable.

When we approached the vendors, they dropped the bombshell that the price was listed wrongly and they wanted closer to $295,000. But after checking with the bank, Jim and I agreed to go to $265,000, and the worst and cheapest block in the valley was officially ours.

Everything was falling into place as we settled into our new home. It may have been far from perfect but, as they say, it had potential. Our capacity to take in unwanted animals, to rehabilitate them and rehome them was great, and Jim, whose day job was as an electrician, was on a steep learning curve. Nothing fazed him. He was an absolute natural. With extra flat acreage loaned by some local property investors for supplementary horse grazing, we were soon officially named Pakuratahi Farm Animal Sanctuary, and in charge of a number of old and wonky farm animals and horses.

Of course there were the usual adjustments which come from two households coming together. Poor Leah was only five but you could almost see the horror on her face when I turned up to school to collect her and her brother every second week in my 6-tonne horse truck that we had purchased for a great price from a horsey lady. (It was an upgrade from the old home-built float that was on its last wheels and perfect for my animal wrangling jobs.) The other parents drove nice cars down the cul-de-sac to the suburban middle-class primary school, but not me; I drove the big blue TK Bedford truck. It was Leah's first year at school and she was very specific about what she liked. She liked pink clothes, she always liked to be organised and on time, and she liked meat not vegetables. The pink clothes I could do, but the rest was not quite our reality. With the food we compromised. Jim and I were both now vegan but we made the kids vegetarian meals that they enjoyed, much to their surprise. Shaun was much easier going, more of a people pleaser. If those around him were smiling or, better still, laughing then his job was done and he was happy.

After school one day we arranged to meet Jim at his mother's house. Grandma Carly had been a rock in the kids' lives. She had helped Jim survive the scary and lonely act of solo parenting when it was his week with the kids, and Leah and Shaun loved to spend time with her. So with all the recent upheaval and change we'd often use her as a meeting point after school.

On one particular day I had run out of bird seed for Gerber and needed to pop by the local pet store on the way to Carly's. We had been to this store many times before for supplies and had never been impressed. It smelt dank and the large fish tank in the middle of the floor had such a huge fish in it, it didn't have much room to move. As I looked at the parrot treats, Shaun and Leah made their way through the screen door into another room at the back of the shop where the birds, puppies and kittens were kept. They always seemed to have a fresh supply of baby animals out the back.

The children hadn't been away from my side for long when I felt a tugging at my leg.

'The puppy is hurt, Carolyn.'

Shaun looked concerned so I dropped what I was doing and followed him into the back room. The noise of the one hundred or so budgies, finches and parakeets was deafening, and the smell was worse than the rank odour at the front of the shop. It was more an overpowering stench of faeces—bird, cat and dog—with a heavy splash of matured urea. Shaun and Leah pointed into the back corner of an old aviary. There sat a tiny little tri-coloured corgi cross favouring her little front paw. I looked at the pup and then I looked at the sign that read 'Border collie $50'.

'But she's not a Border collie,' I questioned the attendant who had walked in to see if she could help us.

'Oh yes, she absolutely is,' she assured me with confidence.

'Crossed with corgi?' I pushed.

'No, she's a Border collie.'

Unsatisfied, but knowing I was getting nowhere, I decided to change my line of questioning. 'So why is she holding her paw up?'

'Oh someone stood on her. The vet is coming this afternoon to decide if she is worth keeping.'

My jaw dropped and the kids stepped in closer. 'What do you mean?' I asked.

The upbeat young attendant lowered her voice and said that they didn't keep the sick ones.

I looked at Shaun and Leah and thought about our lovely new home. We had just rehomed the last of our rescue dogs and Murphy could do with a friend.

'So what do you think, Shaun, are you responsible enough to care for a puppy?'

His eyes widened as I placed the little fat stumpy-legged pup into his arms and we walked towards the checkout.

At Grandma Carly's we tossed around names and eventually settled on Haggis. Haggis McKenzie, the perfect name for a dumpy little corgi cross.

I took a moment to worry about Haggis's siblings. What if their new families had truly believed they were Border collies, what if they felt cheated or disappointed in some way, how would that bode for the puppies? I assured myself that if they were anything like Haggis the families would surely realise how lucky they were . . . but I couldn't help but think that both the dogs and the families had been set up to fail by the dishonest pet store. This store has since been sold and has new owners.

CHAPTER 9

An unconventional marriage

Jim and I planned to wed a few months after we had moved into our new home.

We had organised a very simple affair; we wanted to be married at home with 30 or so family and friends, nothing flash, just a day filled with love.

Although Jim's wife had left him a year or two before we met, they hadn't actually got around to signing the divorce papers, so six weeks before the wedding Jim set the paperwork in motion. He signed and paid for his half and passed the other half on to his soon-to-be ex-wife so the document could be completed and filed before our chosen date. We were so excited and so wrapped up in the approaching festivities that it wasn't until a week before the big event that we realised we had not received confirmation of Jim's divorce.

'You'll never believe it,' said Jim as he walked pale-faced into the room.

'What's up?' His expression had me a little worried. Jim had just got off the phone to his ex-wife. Except she wasn't his ex-wife, not even close. She hadn't filed the paperwork.

'But why?' My eyes widened as I did a quick countdown in my head. Yip, only five days to our wedding. This was not looking good.

'She said I owe her money.' Jim shook his head. 'I told her we were going to pay it off, we just don't have it right now.'

When Jim's wife left him, he had decided to stay in their home to keep things as stable as possible for Shaun and Leah. At the time, her lawyers had contacted Jim requiring him to sign a document stating that upon selling the house his wife would get a percentage of the profits. But where it all went pear-shaped was that Jim agreed on a fixed fee; they decided on the amount he would pay her based on a valuation they got at the time. Jim's wife agreed to leave her share in until the house was sold, as it was still very much the children's home, but more than two years later the market had dropped and when he sold it, the price he had received was nowhere near the original valuation. Jim had done everything he could to keep his children settled in their home and now he owed his ex-wife money we just didn't have. She was right, though, we did owe her. It was in the contract Jim had signed, but as the house had only just sold, the details of the payment hadn't really been discussed yet. We just had no idea that she would pounce on us from out of the blue.

'So what did she say exactly?' I was strangely calm.

Jim looked bewildered as he repeated the conversation that clearly had him blindsided. 'She said, "Ha, ha, I haven't signed the papers, so you'll have to cancel your wedding."'

I sat with Haggis on my knee stretched out like a sunbathing otter. 'Crikey, I didn't realise we were playing games.'

So Jim and I brainstormed. We were about to be paid for the sale of my bus so that was the money issue settled; we would clear that debt immediately. Next issue: what about the wedding? Well, we decided we didn't need a piece of paper to confirm our love and commitment to each other, so after a quick call to the marriage celebrant it was decided that we would have a commitment ceremony instead. And with Haggis as my bouquet, Murphy as Jim's wingman, Shaun, Leah, family and friends surrounding us and the motley crew looking up from the paddock, that's just what we did.

There was so much love around the ceremony. Two days earlier I had celebrated my thirty-first birthday, and had woken that morning to find Jim missing. As I yawned and stretched I saw a note on my pillow with a very messy message saying, 'Look out the window'. So I did, and there in the paddock, on our disastrous new arena, lay a giant love note configured from old car tyres: 'Happy Bday CP I Love You'. As my eyes searched the paddock, seeking out the artist, there he was walking up the steep driveway towards me, head to toe black as soot, with a beaming white smile directed straight at me.

So that's why, even today, if someone asks me my name I have to ask why they are asking. My legal name is still Carolyn Press, but I prefer to use Carolyn Press-McKenzie. It may not be completely legal, but I decided that day that I was not going to let a silly situation sabotage my wish to carry Jim's name. We have built a life together and I want it to be known that he is part of my journey and what better way than to take his name as my own. Jim and his ex did eventually divorce, years later, so she could remarry, and he signed without fuss, in fact with great delight. We still haven't married officially, because for us the funny little commitment ceremony on our little hill with our family, friends and animals was perfect, and all we will ever need.

CHAPTER 10

Three horses, a goose and a common weed

The motley crew were in bliss with 13 acres to amble around.

They stuck together as an inseparable tribe, welcoming all the newcomers with helpful and non-judgemental ease. Drum the Clydesdale stayed his reliable calm self as new horses were transported into our care. The majority of them were either injured and deemed expendable or elderly and consequently forgotten. We worked alongside the SPCA rescuing local horses in need that had all been failed in one way or another. Each story was about people giving up on them, not able or wanting to provide what the horses so desperately needed. Although my vet nursing skills and obsessive dedication to wound healing were invaluable, their emotional states were inevitably what needed the most work.

One day the SPCA called with a horrific story. A man had allegedly attacked and raped a small herd of three horses. The owner lived out of town and the horses needed somewhere safe to rest their beaten and stressed bodies. We collected the two mares and a filly that day. The older mare had been chased but not caught; she had, however, fallen down a drain. The SPCA team needed help to get this exhausted horse out safely. The chestnut mare and her foal had been violated.

This man was known to police and his telltale signs of tampering had first been noticed in the stables at the local race track, but more recently he had been braving the elements and picking older or more vulnerable horses on surprisingly public road sides. The mess he left was always the same: the horses beside themselves, anxious and on edge, not wanting to be handled or touched. Their rear ends would be covered in engine oil, the lucky ones would have superficial wounds and the not-so-lucky had deep and severe wounds. Horses that were younger were more severely damaged, perhaps because they fought harder and had been restrained with more force. Word got around town that the perpetrator was at it again and more tampered-with mares were being discovered. For those who thought to call the police it was always too late. One owner told me that in addition to the wounds around the horse's rear, her mare had broken out in stress hives which had started to slough. Her horse was a toxic mess, which the vet put down to the severe emotional trauma.

Laboratory tests confirmed that engine oil was present on the horses, but frustratingly there was never any firm forensic evidence, and today this man still walks free.

Of the two beautiful mares and one filly that we took in and rehabilitated, two were returned to the owner who moved them to grazing out of the area. But the most damaged, a stunning seventeen-year-old thoroughbred called Lady, was signed over to us for further rehabilitation and eventual rehoming. We treasured and adored her and made sure she felt safe. When her sores finally healed we found her just the right forever home. She is still there today.

The more injured animals Jim and I were faced with the more we knew we needed to help. My vet nursing skills were extremely useful, but I couldn't help thinking that I could be doing more. We had seen vets shake their heads over and over again saying, 'No, sadly there is just nothing more that can be done' or 'You've tried your best, but it's too costly to go to the next stage of treatment and to be honest it's just not worth it'. I was really starting to resent this no-can-do attitude. I remembered the never-say-no philosophy that I lived by when I was working on movies, where I made the choice to think outside the square and come up with a solution that kept everyone happy and made the project plausible. And I couldn't help wondering why we couldn't apply that attitude to rescue and rehabilitation work.

My friends had been telling me about a woman who taught the art of healing with herbal remedies. Apparently she was amazing and had a farm crammed with medicinal herbs. I was intrigued and arranged to go to meet her. From that first encounter, I was totally in awe of her wisdom. I enrolled in her one-year diploma course in herbal remedies, and on completion I enrolled in the advanced second year. I was a sponge. Who knew nature could be such a powerful healer? Well, actually I did.

I remember one summer holiday when my brothers and I were teenagers. David had slipped and fallen down a waterfall, as you do. His wrist was severely broken and in the months that followed, the doctors told my parents that the bone was not healing and that David would need a surgical graft from his thigh bone to his wrist. My mum was an amazing lady, calm and loving and quietly determined, and had an unbeatable knack for making everything okay. All throughout our childhood we wanted for nothing; it wasn't about having money or possessions. The magic that Mum wove into our lives was about being positive, being determined and having a huge can-do attitude. Mum decided to put her upbeat philosophy into action to help my brother in this situation, and set about finding a way to heal David's damaged wrist despite the doctor's diagnosis.

She had only three weeks until David's scheduled surgery, but she had a plan. She had taken my brother to a naturopath and had a list of foods and remedies that would help the bone to mend. So Mum set about making sugar-free nutritional meals packed with nuts and seeds, massaged all of David's limbs daily, wrapped his broken limb with comfrey poultices, and twice a day plunged the injured wrist in and out of hot and cold water. I watched and marvelled.

The day of the scheduled surgery came all too quickly. Mum and David bundled themselves off to hospital, ready to accept the worst with a positive smile. David was sitting up in his hospital bed awaiting the pre-anaesthetic drugs when the doctor entered the room scratching his head. He was holding the pre-surgical X-rays of David's wrist. He glanced past my mother's nervous smile and rested his eyes on David's arm, then he scratched his head some more.

As the X-ray was slipped onto the lightbox he explained. 'This was an absolute non-healer. But I'll be damned if it hasn't gone and healed itself.'

Mum beamed at the doctor, whose words were music to her ears, and David beamed at Mum. They could breathe again. Mum's can-do attitude—the one that never let us down—had come up trumps again.

As the years passed I never forgot the miracle that Mum's

problem-solving and determination produced. I also didn't forget that although the doctor's advice and treatment plan was fair and sound it was not the only solution or, as it turned out, the best way forward for my brother. I learnt that even when a medical professional isn't wrong, it also doesn't mean that they are right. I learnt not to just accept an opinion or a conclusion if you didn't like it, but to dig deeper, try harder and to look for alternatives.

And though I wasn't conscious of it at the time, David's unplanned trip down that waterfall completely changed the way I chose to live my life. Which brings me to my next story.

It was like a scene from a horror movie. I was used to being called out to assist animals in crisis, but I wasn't used to coming home and finding my own charges in that state.

We had been asked to take in some geese because apparently the father goose was attacking human visitors. On questioning his owners about why they thought this was happening, they drew a complete blank. Their response was that he was just a bad goose, in fact a bad egg, and they no longer wanted him. I asked them about his home life and if they could identify when he played up the most.

They pondered this and said, 'It's probably when his wife is sitting on eggs.'

'So how many other geese do you have?' I enquired.

'Well, there is the male, his wife, the three male goslings she last hatched and the three eggs she is sitting on now.'

I explained that pilgrim ganders are particularly protective during breeding season, and he probably had the weight of the world on his shoulders with such a large family to watch over. But the human father insisted that he had had enough and in the usual blackmailing fashion we were getting used to, he told us if we did not take the male geese then they were going in the pot. After further conversations the man stood firm in his decision. The mum goose was settled with her eggs and he was reluctant to let her go. It's an awful feeling breaking up a family. But dad and the boys needed to leave the property or they would be dead. So we took the bachelor family and strongly suggested to the owner that he collect any future eggs so the cycle would not continue. We settled the gaggle of boys in and set about learning what made them tick. To be honest it was an easy transition and not an aggressive honk was heard between them.

On this day as I came up our driveway I could see that the animals were unsettled, and when I stepped out of the truck I noticed a trail of blood. My eyes followed the bright red puddles and drips to Orlando, one of the young geese. He had collapsed in the grass and the back of his neck was non-existent. The flesh had been ripped away and what was left was a mess of muscle and veins, with sneak peeks at an exposed vertebrae. I bundled the still breathing young bird into the truck and raced back into town.

'No, there's nothing we can do, he's a goner,' was the opinion of the vet on duty. I could see where he was coming from; it truly wasn't a pretty sight to behold and to imagine a way out of this horrendous pickle would require a good stretch of the imagination. But it has to be said that imagination is one thing I am not short of.

'What do you think, Jim?' I felt guilty making the vet wait for my answer while I called Jim on the phone, but my gut told me to hesitate. 'I know it's awful, the hawk has done a real number on this little guy, but I think I can heal him.'

Jim processed what he knew of the situation 'So he has no skin covering his neck? And you can see the bone?'

'Yes,' I confirmed. 'The wound's about the size of a crab apple.'

'Well, what do you think?' Jim passed it back to me.

I thought about it. I had just successfully mended the broken leg of one of the local huntmaster's best horses. He was going to be fed to the dogs, but a friend of mine had told the huntmaster to give me and my herbal remedies a try. The horse had been transported to our block and within months was ready for light work again. I knew that I had the ability to heal damaged bones and tissue, but was I brave enough to try this wound? I wasn't sure. It wasn't the work involved that made me hesitate, it was the quality of life for the goose. Was I just prolonging Orlando's suffering while I indulged my own selfish curiosity?

I decided to give it a go. The vet was not at all convinced but allowed me to take the bird on the condition that we put an axe through its neck at the first sign of decline. I stocked up on pain relief and antibiotics and headed out the door.

I already had some comfrey tincture in my cupboard but needed to make a healing oil. So as I wandered through the paddocks, I politely asked the plants for permission to pick their leaves. I know it must sound mad, but that is the way I was taught and to be honest it felt nice to stick with the tradition of being grateful for the harvest.

Plantain is my most favourite herb in the whole world. No, not the green bananas, but the common weed that you walk over every day on your front lawn. This little guy is taken for granted by most New Zealanders, but is one of the most useful herbs that I have ever had the pleasure to work with.

It is also known as snakeweed in Africa because of its abilities to draw poison or foreign objects from a wound. I was so obsessed with plantain that when on school trips with Leah I would encourage the kids to make their own plantain spit wads when suffering from a graze, a bee sting, an insect bite, a nettle sting or a splinter. I'd show them how to pick a fresh leaf, chew it up and, hey presto, they'd have a 'spit poultice'. Apply to the affected area, wait a few minutes, and problem solved!

But mostly I loved plantain because it is such a dramatic and effective cellular regenerator while at the same time drawing out trapped infection. It contains a compound called allantoin, which is also found in comfrey, a snail's trail and the urine of many mammals. In science research, allantoin is extracted and used to promote cell proliferation, and it is incredibly good at healing wounds. I had used plantain poultices, tinctures, creams and oils on my family and the sanctuary animals very successfully, and was always stunned and thrilled with the results.

An infused oil of plantain is easy peasy to make and a great basic to have on hand. After washing and drying the leaves I tore and scrunched them up and then immersed them in the top layer of a double boiler containing first-pressed, cold-pressed olive oil. After six hours the extraction of the healing compounds into the oil was complete. I strained out the spent plant material and smiled as I poured the golden green oil into a clean jar.

For the first few weeks Orlando the goose was cared for in our lounge, where he received antibiotics and pain relief. I set about drizzling the plantain-infused oil on his wound. I had added a few extra goodies such as St John's wort for topical pain, borage as an anti-inflammatory, rosehip for scarring and manuka as an antimicrobial to the mix. It was working, the wound started to granulate and with physio by way of gentle laps around a lavender-infused bath—our bath—Orlando was back to normal and fully feathered within six weeks. In fact, you'd never know he had ever been attacked; emotionally and physically he was back in top form.

After that attack, we hung flags from our fence posts to deter the hawks. That year had been a particularly bad year for hawk food and neighbours even reported the desperate birds flying off with chickens in their clutches. We often see them hanging around, but whatever made them so bold that year seems to have passed, and they haven't needed to brave our land for food again, for which we are extremely grateful.

CHAPTER 11

A knack for learning

My first boss hired me because I was the only applicant for the trainee veterinary nurse position who didn't reply to his question about why they wanted the job with, 'Because I love animals'.

I had said, 'Because I want to learn'.

I was only sixteen years old and although I had failed most of my school exams, I had a real knack for learning. I was terrible at retaining anything I'd read in a book. The only way I could learn was from real-life experience. So, for two years I listened to my boss interacting with clients, I watched his manner and technique with patients and I studied my trade at night school. As it was really just him and me at the small but busy suburban vet clinic, I was able to learn from being involved in every part of every animal's journey. But after two years it started to feel a little like solitary confinement. I had qualified as a vet nurse and at the tender age of nineteen

I started to wonder if there was more to life. The next six years were a jumble of cramming in as many experiences as I could.

I went from working at a law firm to a job as an assistant to Sir Bob Jones, which involved a diverse range of tasks, including serving him his meat pies on ZKRJI, his little blue private jet, until a broken leg in full plaster for nine months saw me bored and back at school topping up my science knowledge. I followed this with a blast through the corporate wonderland that was Fay Richwhite Merchant Bankers in the early 1990s and on to a hospitality course that led me to bar tending. Vet nursing and care-giving gave me my ticket around the world, with an eight-week stint in Africa allowing just enough time for me to be dragged into an alleyway and mugged by seven young men with knives. With no money I had to hitchhike by myself across five African countries, and survive some pretty hairy adventures, much to my poor parents' horror. Then it was a quick stint as a cocktail waitress on a cruise ship, crossing the triangle from New York to Bermuda several times, before I staged a walkout over poor working conditions and was finally deported back to Wellington where I settled into Central Wellington Vets as their senior surgical nurse. The team at Central Wellington were my home and family for three years before I set off with Leon and marriage number one.

Looking back, I loved everything about Central Wellington Vets . . . and I still do. The hands-on experience was invaluable; as senior nurse I was abreast of all aspects of the animal's treatment. I was the anaesthetist, the radiographer and the lab technician. I took bloods, lanced abscesses and descaled teeth. I comforted clients, pondered behavioural issues and on more than one occasion slept all night with the paw of a poisoned dog in my hand so I would know the moment they started to wake from a drug-induced coma and if they were starting to convulse again.

The most important lesson I took from Central was that

anything is achievable if you dig deep and try hard. From time to time we would have clients who had given up on their animals. Maybe it was inappropriately spraying around the home, or maybe it needed expensive surgery, but after a pleading smile to my boss and a nod from my boss to the client, the animal would be signed over to us and I was allowed the freedom to organise whichever treatment or surgery it needed and then find it a wonderful new and understanding home. Usually I would find if you changed the animal's environment by rehoming it carefully, the problem would disappear. Or if it needed surgery, maybe to have a leg amputated or similar, it would just attract a more dedicated and sympathetic sort of home. Central Wellington Vets allowed me to develop my natural instincts and ability to problem-solve, and I loved every minute of it.

So when I told my boss Mike that it was time for me to leave and start a new chapter in my life, I cried. He simply looked me in the eye and said, 'Carolyn, if there's one thing I have learnt in this life, it's that no one is indispensable.' I knew he really meant that I would be missed, but life goes on—and he was right. I had left behind the world's best job and the world's best workmates to get married and pursue my passion for animal training and behaviour. The team at Central will always be family to me and even now, years later, if I am ever in a pickle they are the ones who I trust with the lives of my loved ones.

Fast forwarding through the years, we were all now settled at Pakuratahi Farm Animal Sanctuary, and Jim and I were both working full-time to pay the bills.

Jim was working as a fire alarm design engineer and I had taken a position as a locum veterinary nurse at the Wellington SPCA. I was so excited; imagine working in an environment where saving lives and finding happy ever afters was the whole point. I naively thought that I was about to enter a romantic world of loveliness.

A few weeks earlier Jim had taken my big stinky 4x4 'off roading' on our land. I'd asked him not to because I was pretty attached to the old beast and in a killjoy sort of a way did not consider it a toy for his pleasure. Of course it got stuck. It was stuck beyond your wildest stucks and there was no access for another vehicle to get it out until the land dried in summer. So with a new job and no car, I took my neighbour up on a very kind offer and bought her retro Lada station wagon. Hmmm, it wasn't exactly my top pick to cruise in; it was really heavy though much to the kids' delight it had this knack of bouncing as I drove.

My first day at the SPCA started with more of a thump than a bounce.

'But I am a locum nurse, it shouldn't matter to you if I get burnt out, I'm not your problem.' I was on the verge of begging the acting CEO of the SPCA to let me keep four little abandoned pups. I was walking a fine line, trying to stay professional and yet trying to convince my boss that he was wrong. Just an hour earlier these pups had been picked up and brought into the shelter. They were weak and cold and I needed to set to work feeding and supporting them immediately. But as bad luck would have it, the acting CEO walked into the tired old cluttered clinic room just as I was taking them out of the cage.

He looked the small bundles up and down, dropped his chin and shook his head in remorse saying it was a shame they were too young and would have to be put to sleep.

I looked at him with a professionally masked horror. 'Why?' I asked.

In a sympathetic tone he started to reason with me. 'We have rules and our rules state that puppies this young are just not viable.'

'Why?' I asked again.

'Well, they are just too time consuming. We can't afford staff getting exhausted or sick.'

'But I am not staff. I am qualified and I am available and ready to care for these puppies.'

As I pitched my case some of the full-time staff rallied around me for support, or so I thought. As I looked to them for reassurance, I saw the same defeated look. Chins dropped and heads shaking, they took the pups from my grasp and set about euthanising them. I was gobsmacked.

Still trying to stay professional I busied myself cleaning surgical instruments ready for sterilisation. My eyes had welled with tears and I felt very helpless and alone. A million questions were running through my brain. How could no one else see how tremendously unjust this was? Why would an entire staff just accept and comply with these rules? Surely they could see it was wrong? Where was their fight?

Later that day I was sat down for a debrief. I was told that it wasn't our fault that the pups died, it was society's, the ignorant people who didn't desex their dog, and the cruel losers who dumped them.

Nope, I wasn't buying it. Those pups needed us; their lives were literally in our hands. Forget the blame game. The puppies weren't responsible for their situation and they had perfectly viable little lives . . . and now because of a lot of rules and excuses they were dead.

One thing I have learnt about myself over the years is that I can't read very well. It's an odd thing as I clearly love to write. I remember back in primary school we would have colour-coded reading cards with a story on one side and several comprehension questions on the other. The problem would start when the teacher gave us 30 minutes to read the stories and answer the questions. I'd go clammy and panic. I'd try to start reading from left to right as I had been taught, but my annoying eyes would fly off to the right-hand side of the page and start reading backwards, something over which I had absolutely no control. I was ten years old and maybe that was the first time I had really been put under pressure to read. But the more I needed to keep up with the class, the more I would panic and race to the end and work backwards. So I learned to cheat. Not cheating in the write-100-times-on-the-blackboard 'I must not cheat' way, but more a self-preservation and 'learning to work within my limitations' way. Instead of fighting my backward programmed brain, I'd go straight to the list of questions and look for key words. How many sheep did the shepherd shear? I'd just scan the page for the words shear, sheep or shepherd and only concentrate on that sentence. And so far it's worked.

With reading being a sticking point I didn't really take the time to delve into animal behaviour books. I had a reasonable understanding from my vet nursing studies and I watched and listened to the experts and owners around me, but the most important penny-dropping moment for me was when I realised that all the latest trends and techniques from all over the world could not compete with, not even touch the sides of, good old-fashioned common sense. And when coupled with patience, determination and empathy there was really no behaviour problem that could remain unsolved.

So I'd like to believe that by not reading every behaviour book in town, I was able to develop my own intuition and instinct. My mind was less cluttered and I could go about my business with a relatively fresh and untampered approach. All of which was about to come in handy.

CHAPTER 12

Head dog handler

When my stint as a locum nurse had finished at the SPCA, they invited me to apply for the position of head dog handler.

I completely immersed myself in the role and set about making changes. When I had first taken the job all of the nine or so dogs kennelled at the SPCA were expected to exercise together and to get along. If a fight broke out then the perpetrator would be euthanised. With the SPCA being such a highly charged and reactive environment I chose to implement another system: to rotate smaller, more compatible exercising groups. The system worked well.

I introduced fun and enriching training programmes such as clicker training, mini agility courses, hide and seek games and hand signal training. We also began to use Halti head harnesses when walking the dogs so they learnt to defer to their human companion and not to pull on the lead. We gave massages to our more stressed-out charges—some of whom were addicted to adrenaline—which calmed them down and released endorphins. I was also grateful that at the time of my employment the SPCA's board members had just approved a dog walking programme, something that had never been allowed in the past. Things were looking up in the battered old shelter. The powers-that-be were accepting that things needed to change and the animals were certainly benefiting from it.

One morning I arrived at the kennels extra early, in the hope of getting my head around the day before it started. No sooner had I put my bag down than I noticed a new face in the line-up. His head was low and he looked stoically unengaged among all the chaos and barking. I read the chart attached to the front of his kennel, which said the inspectors had brought him in to the shelter during the night. Apparently his owner had been pulled over in his car by the police and when the officers had carried out a routine search they had found this inwardly staunch dog trapped in the boot of the sedan. The guy was detained by the police for drug-related issues and the dog was taken to the SPCA.

I looked down at the dog in front of me—still no reaction to the environment. It was too early to ascertain whether his subdued demeanour was acceptance or denial. One more glance over his kennel chart told me that he was to be held in SPCA custody until a court hearing, or until he was signed over or returned to his owner. In the meantime, the name slot on his chart was empty. As I kept reading I found out that this impressive dog had been trapped in the car boot all the way from Taupo to Wellington—almost 400 kilometres. That was it. I grabbed a pen and in the blank name slot I carefully wrote the word 'Taupo'.

Taupo was one of those dogs that anyone would stop and look at twice. Although this big tan Staffy cross was impressively muscular and would absolutely be the pride of any tryhard's collection of staunch animals, I noticed that even in this high-pressure situation he wasn't baring his teeth and foaming at the mouth. Far from it, he was quietly minding his own business, staying out of trouble and just existing.

For the first few days I didn't really lay a hand on Taupo. I would open his run, allowing him access to the outside yard where he would sniff about, poo and pee and wait to be let into his kennel again. Probably due to a slight fear of the unknown, I had chosen to go with the formula of quietly allowing us to suss each other out with no pressure, which mostly had worked in the past for these types of tough-guy dogs. Seized dogs were often different from the usual family pets that came into the shelter. Although the environment was stressful for all incoming dogs, often seized dogs dealt with the stress in a different way. The sort of dogs that the inspectors uplifted, pending their owner's possible prosecution, had often been chained and/or abused or were from unkind or ignorant homes. They were the sort of dogs that were emotionally damaged, broken or angry and usually more edgy as they were mostly not desexed. They had been through the wringer by the time they were placed in the custody of the SPCA.

I would watch the seized dogs come and go and I learnt not to handle them as I would the family pets. Seeing their scared and reactive behaviour, my instincts would tell me just to leave them be and to allow them the time they needed to accept their new environment. I would watch them watching me. I was calm and reliable, I tended to their needs and I placed no pressure on them. There were big signs all over their kennels 'keep out', 'do not handle' and 'dog handler only'.

Taupo and I got into a rhythm; he learnt to trust and anticipate my movements and after just five days of detoxing from his old life he subtly wagged his tail when I approached. I smiled and gently offered the back of my hand for him to sniff and then it happened—he looked at me! His big brown eyes were gentle and relaxed. It was the first time since his arrival that Taupo had made any eye contact, the first time he had acknowledged me. So for the first time Taupo and I went out into the yard together, he walked off to have a pee and a poo and I sat down on a wooden platform with my back to him. A few minutes later we were both sitting on the platform side by side, not talking, not touching, just sitting and enjoying the sun as it shone down on our backs. I could feel the emotion of this amazingly stoic dog. People had not treated him with respect in the past and yet he had such a capacity to cope and remain indifferent—I couldn't help but respect him. And as he leaned into me I knew the feeling was mutual.

The scary thing about forming a relationship with a seized dog is that their destiny is completely out of your control. Sometimes the cases make it all the way to court, and the ideal outcome is of course that the owners are prosecuted and made to be accountable for whatever cruel or heinous act they have inflicted on the animal. Sometimes there is no court hearing, but the inspectors still manage to have the dog signed over to the SPCA. And sometimes the inspectors just can't make a case stick or get the owners to hear reason and the animal has to be returned to its former unsafe life. As the dog handler I very quickly learnt that in many cases none of the above outcomes were ideal for the animals, not even the wins.

When I first started work at the SPCA my colleagues told me of a beautiful and gentle pitbull terrier that had been seized by the inspectors. She had been treated very badly, was malnourished, emaciated and pregnant and there was a very strong prosecution pending. Over the best part of a year they nurtured the mum dog, and she gained weight and confidence, giving birth to eight healthy pups. Because there was a court case pending, neither the mum nor her pups could leave the shelter; they were essentially just waiting in the system as wards of the court until an outcome was reached.

Finally the day came and the inspectors celebrated when they won the case. She was officially free from the abuse, and her puppies, who had grown up in the shelter, would finally be able to move on to find safe and loving lives of their own.

But that's when reality hit. The staff all knew the rules and probably should have seen it coming a mile away, but the blissful denial they chose to live with was blown apart when the orders came from management instructing them to destroy the mum and her babies because they were pitbull terriers and the SPCA did not rehome pitbulls. So after a year of saving this beautiful gentle girl's life, and enriching and teaching her eight amazingly special pups, the staff held them in their arms and sobbed as the dogs shut their eyes for the last time. They were told that at least the mum wouldn't have to suffer anymore. But the thing was they hadn't seen her suffer for an entire year; they had seen her blossom and her true nature shine. She was beautiful on the inside and out, and so were each and every one of her fun-loving puppies.

The day the inspector came down to the kennels to tell me that Taupo's case was not going to court and that he had been signed over to the SPCA, I stopped breathing. Taupo was truly such an amazing soul, but what if no one else saw in him what I did. I talked further to the inspector about Taupo's rehoming options and then made the long walk up the steps to the CEO's office. Thank goodness she respected my opinion.

Her first question was whether I considered Taupo to be a pitbull type.

'No, absolutely not, he's a Staffy cross.'

Did I think he was aggressive in any way?

'No, absolutely not, he is a calm and considerate dog.'

Did I think he was rehomable?

'Yes, absolutely. We could definitely find him a wonderful home.'

And that was that.

Pending a formal temperament assessment that was to be carried out by me, Taupo would be allowed into our rehoming programme. Phew!

Temperament tests are funny things. When I was starting out as a dog handler I completely bought into the hype, going on courses and listening to speakers from America. In my mind if they said it then it must be right. I was young and initially didn't stop for a moment to ponder the realities of what they were asking a dog to do. I learnt that if a dog passed the temperament test it lived and if it failed it would be allowed a second test and if it failed that it died. It was as simple as that.

But the more I worked with the dogs the more I realised that environment plays a huge factor in a dog's temperament and ability to cope. And a shelter environment was more than most could bear. The reasons why they acted the way they did or, more to the point, reacted, wasn't about whether they were a 'good' or a 'bad' dog, it was about their coping skills. The same could be said for the cats in the cattery. But in the kennels the tests were so terribly contrived. They even included walking a large terrifyingly creepy doll towards the dog, and if they lashed out, growled or barked at the doll a big black mark went on their temperament test sheet. If they growled or reacted to the plastic hand on the end of a stick that was jerked up and down in their food bowl, same big black mark. Or if they reacted to a staff member running into the compound yelling and waving his or her arms at them, then more black ticks.

It was my job to assess these dogs, but, seriously, the more I saw the wide-eyed and confused looks coming from the dogs, the more I realised that temperament testing was no more than an awful prank played on an unsuspecting victim. Each dog carried heartbreak or pain, so why not allow them the dignity and respect they deserved? Why not give them the time to process their grieving? But in shelters throughout New Zealand the formula was the same, rules and hoops were in place and time was the one thing that these beautiful, confused and desperate animals were very rarely ever allowed.

As part of our rehoming programme, we had just struck up a deal with a dog training school. The head trainers would come into the SPCA a couple of times a week and take some of the dogs off site for some training. I was so pleased to see the nine or so dogs in my care have more opportunities to learn, and I was even more excited that they also had an opportunity to escape the compound for a few hours.

The trainers were lovely ladies, all pepped up with the training buzz. And of course they were following to the letter all of the trends from America. They had been coming only for a couple of weeks and I initially handed them the easier dogs, the ones who had had full and enriched lives before their families moved away or had had human babies and no longer saw a place for a dog in their lives. There were so many reasons that these amazing and intelligent animals had been dumped at the shelter and sadly it was never through any fault of their own.

The ladies would return from the sessions thrilled to bits with progress; the dogs had been angels, interactive and keen to learn tricks. The ladies patted themselves on the back for a job well done and I thanked them for enriching the dogs that day. They had been trying out clicker training, which is a type of positive reinforcement for the dogs, and things were moving along swimmingly. Of course I was very familiar with the benefits of clicker training as I had used it to break down and teach behaviour in my movie work. Clicker training is a great upbeat method that can be taught to any species.

As an aside, I remember one year teaching cows to do kung-fu and aerobics movements for a TV commercial. The clicker training was so effective that the cows just couldn't get enough of it. We made the mistake of leaving their exercise step in the paddock while we took a lunch break. We came out from the barn an hour later to find the girls all lined up on their steps ready and waiting for their treats.

After a few weeks of watching the ladies and watching the dogs, I noticed that the trainers had a real sense of accomplishment about them; with clickers in tow they firmly believed they had this dog behaviour business nailed. So bursting with curiosity as to how they would handle him, I passed over Taupo's lead to one of the trainers. I gave full disclosure, explaining his temperament and his story. I told her that she would need to take her time and get to know him first. So off they went.

I knew Taupo was going to be safe but what I didn't know was if he was going to be understood. So I spent the next few hours with half my mind on the work in front of me and half my mind on Taupo. As the clock struck 3 p.m., in strode the trainers. They looked annoyed.

'What's wrong?' I asked, my eyes searching frantically behind them until they rested on a very disinterested looking Taupo.

'This dog is not safe, I just don't trust him,' replied the trainer. She then went on to explain that he wouldn't look her in the eye, he wouldn't respond to commands, and he wouldn't take a treat. 'We just don't trust him and he is absolutely not suitable for rehoming.'

I explained to the trainers again that Taupo was a very special soul and that although clickers and treats and tricks were a wonderful learning tool for some dogs, Taupo would only work for trust and respect. I suggested that they take him out the next day and just calmly spend time with him, maybe sit with him and breathe. I said that it wasn't about what he could do for them, it was about really opening up and showing him what they could do for him.

The next day the trainers arrived looking concerned. They had been chatting among themselves and felt that I was putting them in a very awkward and unsafe situation. I asked them to trust me and off they went with Taupo. They were gone for hours and I was starting to second-guess my motives—maybe they'd never understand. But at 3.30 p.m. they walked through the doors of the shelter, Taupo at their side, all three of them smiling a tranquil calm smile. It was clear that Taupo had worked his magic.

They started to explain to me how completely they connected with him and what a miracle it was. Speaking to the trainers before the session with Taupo had been like talking to a Kardashian-style dog trainer, all wrapped up in what the new hot trend was and because they knew the latest and hottest they expected all the pegs to fit into their fancy round holes. Talking to them now was as though they had just come out of a meeting with the Dalai Lama. The transformation was incredible. These ladies were so invested in gimmicks and teach-me-quick tricks that they had totally missed the most important part: the realness of the animal, the connection, the uncomplicated truth. But through Taupo's steadfast silence they had learnt to stop talking and to listen.

A few weeks later an amazing woman came into the shelter. Her elderly dog had passed away months earlier and she was ready to love again. She knew at once that Taupo was the dog for her. I watched them connect immediately. It was perfect.

CHAPTER 13

Desperate to belong

Knowing that animal behaviour was my passion, the girls from the SPCA cat run would often call on me to help with an extra tricky case.

One day they asked for advice on an extremely timid cat, Patsy, that they had recently rehomed. The new family were super lovely, but were seriously reconsidering their choice of feline companion as they very rarely got to see her. She had been in their home for nearly five months and spent most of her time hiding under the bed. When she was let outside for the first time she went bush immediately and days later they had to set a trap to bring her back home. They wanted to know if there was any hope. After pondering the question for a short while, I asked if I could speak to the owners. I asked them if Patsy ever popped her head out from under the bed when people were present and they replied that she was only ever brave enough if there was food. I smiled. There was our window of hope—food.

So I set about explaining the concept of reward-based clicker training to the family. Stage one was to condition Patsy to the sound the clicker made. I explained it was much like Pavlov's theory: when Patsy heard the clicker I wanted her to think food over fear. My hope was that over time, through exposure to her surroundings, she would desensitise and be able to function as a relatively normal cat in constant search of pleasure. I asked them to click as she ate her meals. The motive here was to get Patsy to associate food with the clicking sound. I then asked them to put morsels of Patsy's favourite food on the floor at the foot of the bed and click when she bravely reached out to get it. After a while the family were able to click the clicker and Patsy would pop her head out from under the bed in anticipation of the reward. They would then offer her food and click again when she bravely took it.

Soon they were playing games with Patsy. One of the owners would hide around the corner or in the wardrobe or up the stairs and click and Patsy would shyly but surely come looking for them. As well as offering her her favourite food the family would tickle and stroke Patsy which she was starting to allow them to do without flinching; in fact purring was becoming her new normal. Finally Patsy's confidence was so great in the home that she would bat the family with her paws to initiate the game and the food and the pats.

My theory was that Patsy rated food over all else, even fear. I had been working the family to a point where they could eventually let her outside. What had gone so wrong in the past was that when outside Patsy would be so overcome with fear that once she found her way into the bush at the end of the garden she was just not brave enough to find her way back. But with the clicker promising her food, safety and love there was no stopping her bounding in through the back door.

Jake the dog had been signed over to the SPCA because the family just couldn't keep him on their property. They owned a motel so there was plenty going on and yet as soon as his owner's back was turned he was up and over the 1.8-metre-high fence. His usual routine was to cross a few main roads and head for the river where he would meet up with other dogs and play for hours and then head back home to the motel for dinner. Lately Jake's owners had resorted to chaining him. They were all miserable.

I asked his owner if she engaged with Jake, or was he just left to his own devices. She explained that although she was essentially working from home at the motel she really didn't spend a lot of time with him. I prescribed a change of routine, where she would allow him to become more involved in her day at the motel and that she should give him little jobs to do, to help him feel included and valued. Jake's owner should also take him to a park or the river herself so that they could enjoy the experience together, but on her terms. Only a week or so later Jake's owner called back. She just didn't have the time to try the tasks and she was in a constant state of worry as to his whereabouts as he was now slipping the collar and chain. So the very next day Jake found himself sitting in kennel number 7 at the Wellington SPCA.

At the time we were swamped, having just taken in seven deaf Dalmatians from a backyard breeder. I was working with them, teaching hand signals until way past my home time. With still so much paperwork to do I knew that I was about to be the only one left in the old shabby building. A little nervous to be lurking the corridors on my own at night, I asked Jake if he would mind joining me at my desk upstairs.

What a gorgeous dog. He was a gentle-looking soul, predominantly huntaway, very leggy, very intelligent and only about two years old. Even though we had only just met, he trotted next to me, off-lead, through the maze of doors and corridors until we reached my desk. He settled at my feet as I worked, looking just as content and relieved as I was to have a companion. As the hours passed and the work was finally done, I settled Jake back in his kennel. I leaned down and, with his chin cupped gently in my hand, looked into his deep intelligent brown eyes and promised him that I would find him his happiness.

The next day I was rostered to start work a little later. As I walked down the driveway to the front entrance of the shelter, to my complete surprise, there was Jake wagging his tail and extremely pleased to see me. He had escaped. In all my time at the shelter, Jake was the first dog I had ever known to escape the compound. It was impressive, but more than just a little bit worrying.

As Jake and I entered the building one of the staff, who was far from impressed with my let's-save-them-all attitude, was quick to remind me that we would be better to put an animal to sleep than to put it back out into the community where it could cause an accident. Of course I kindly disagreed and said I would find a way to keep everyone safe and happy, while acknowledging that we did have huge responsibility to place dogs in the community and that I was, and always would, take that very seriously. I pondered a while for the best solution.

I found Jake amazing. In fact, I'd go so far as to say outstanding. There was no doubt in my mind he was a special dog with that can-do attitude I admired so much in all creatures. His life to date had been boring and had had little enrichment, but instead of sitting around stressing about it, he had found a way to improve it all on his own. Surely that sort of attitude and capability, while not always appropriate, should be recognised and admired. The sad thing was he was now seen as a naughty dog that was too out of control. I just needed to put all that cleverness into the right home. Jake was not a dog that should be or deserved to be overlooked; he needed to feel valued and he needed to be an involved part of a family, not just an annoying afterthought. Seeing him outside the confines of the shelter that day, I was looking at a dog who just wanted to connect. He wanted to please and he wanted to be seen.

I knew if he kept escaping at the shelter then I would be pressured to dispose of him, and, if you know me at all by now, you'll know I was more likely to walk out with him trotting at my side than to send him to heaven for simply being so desperate to belong.

Well, as the saying goes, timing is everything. My friend Vicky the vet called that morning to ask if I knew of a great family dog for some friends who had moved to a new lifestyle block. Vicky barely had time to put the receiver down when I was on the phone to her friend, digging for more information.

The mother was a retired flight attendant who wanted to spend more time with her young and growing family, so they had bought an old relocated church on several acres of vineyard. They wanted a family dog to be part of every aspect of their lives; they wanted a best friend for their children and a companion for her mum as her husband was often away for work. As I listened to the warmth in her voice I started to get excited. I also loved the fact that getting a dog was something her whole family had discussed and prepared for. They were committed to doing whatever they could to be engaged and attentive parents, and the dog they adopted would be an important family member.

Then, as per protocol, I asked about their fencing. For a moment my heart sank. It was seven wire farm fencing and an absolute doddle for a boy like Jake to escape over. On paper it should have been a no right then and there, but in my heart I knew that no fence would keep this boy home. Maybe being a valued family member might. It was risky and I explained his situation thoroughly to the woman. I also explained that if they were indeed happy to take Jake for a trial and he did run off then we would take him back in a flash. So with my fingers and toes crossed into knots, Jake went on trial to the country. I waited anxiously for news.

He learnt to play with toy tractors with his new little brother and to run alongside big tractors with his adoring new dad. He would fondly sit at his new mum's feet as she did the accounts or put another load of washing out and he snuggled on the sofa in between loving arms as the family settled in to watch the telly for the evening.

The updates that came in over the first year reported that Jake was the perfect family dog: loyal, loving, amazing with the children and a wonderful companion for the mum and dad. He never did run away, not even once. Several years later I was thrilled to get another update. I felt a little teary as they told me his favourite spot was sitting on the deck looking over his land and attentively watching his children playing. Jake had found his forever home. His safety fence was not made of wood, not at all, it was made of something much stronger and greater: it was made of love.

CHAPTER 14

Not every dog's normal

My heart melted the moment the inspector placed him in my arms.

Only about six weeks old, he was full of beans and completely oblivious to the fact that only having three functioning legs wasn't every dog's normal.

'Where on earth did you find him?' I was almost whispering as I gently sketched my finger around the outline of his wee deformed fourth leg.

The inspector explained that he had been found asleep in a slipper on a back doorstep in Porirua. The procedure was that we would hold him for seven days to see if anyone came to claim him. If no one showed, this gorgeous little pup's fate was in the hands of the powers-that-be at the shelter.

'Oh dear, what do you want to do with him, Carolyn?' the CEO asked, as I walked into her office still cradling him in my arms. Her eyes fell on his obvious deformity.

'I'd like to take him home, if that's okay?' And so I did.

I named him Napoléon because his little left foreleg was so deformed it reminded me of the classic Napoléon Bonaparte pose, arm placed across his chest and tucked into his jacket. As I told the precious wee fellow his new fancy name, I also informed him that he would be called Ned for short.

Over the next few days I put a lot of thought into whether to amputate Ned's little chicken-wing leg. It was so deformed surely it was useless? But I decided not to rush, to take some time to get to know this sweet little bundle of courage and truly understand how things were for him. As I watched him manoeuvre around over the week ahead, I noticed that he used the leg to lean on and to prop himself up. And to our delight we watched him flap it ever so slightly when he swam. So we decided not to amputate, not yet, not unless it stared to cause him some trouble or if he got it caught on things. As Ned grew, he completely mastered the art of having only one functioning front leg. He'd hop along after Murphy and Haggis, crashing to a halt and always landing on his outstretched chin.

Right from the get-go Ned looked very similar to a kelpie, maybe not pure bred, but kelpie was definitely the top guess of everyone who met him. As Ned's personality revealed itself to us this headstrong and determined little chap started to show some true kelpie behaviours.

I am always amazed and delighted to see how much a dog's breed can help you to understand their nature and quirks. No matter what home, good or bad, no matter what environment, city or country, chained or family pet, and no matter what age, I am yet to meet a golden retriever who doesn't like to lie in puddles. It's instinctive, it's in their genetic make-up, it's who they are. And similarly with Ned, his kelpie-ness meant he absolutely couldn't help himself from nipping passing animals on the backs of their legs or their bottom. He never did it to people but any animal who walked by was fair game.

Although Ned was very active and tried hard to keep up with everyone, you could see that his nipping was partly exaggerated by frustration. As he grew older and slowed down, his good front leg became more arthritic and he in turn became less agile and more exasperated with his disability, but his instincts to want to bite bottoms remained as strong as ever. Of course we trained him out of this behaviour from the beginning; just a glance from us or a well-timed 'Oi, Ned, be nice' when we saw an animal trotting obliviously in his direction was enough for him to flop to his chin with a defeated and guilt-ridden look. He'd then shuffle back away from his target or simply let it pass on by. But to completely erase the thought of bottom-nipping from his mind would have been as impossible as asking a retriever to dislike water.

Over the years I have seen so many dogs in such inap-propriate situations, for instance a one-year-old Siberian husky that came into the SPCA. Her owner, an international student, had purchased her from a pet store. The puppy then lived for that year in the solitude of an apartment, unsocialised, untrained and undesexed. The adolescent dog was dumped at the shelter a week before her owner was due to fly back home to China. Very few of her emotional or physical needs had been met, and she was confused and like a coiled spring. That apartment and that particular owner was night and day from what she needed and the damage was great. Of course we worked our way through her issues, teaching her to trust new people and situations. Because she was a smart girl, she quickly learnt to be a vibrant, strong and athletic husky and was eventually homed with a family who truly understood her needs.

It's easy enough to train dogs to behave a certain way, but you can't change who they are . . . that's innate and it's kind of beautiful. And when choosing a pet it's probably one of the most important things to consider.

CHAPTER 15

Becoming part of the solution

Meanwhile, back at Pakuratahi we were run off our feet.

I was taking home from work the animals who had no safe solution or outcome, like some kittens with ringworm. They just needed time to be medicated and to heal, but because of ringworm's contagious nature, SPCA policy dictated they would be euthanised if they remained at the shelter.

Jim and I were also getting more and more calls about horses, sheep, cows, roosters and pigs that were in trouble. We were working around the clock to keep up. We wanted the animals to be safe and have bright futures, but we were starting to feel a little used. Folk who had made foolish choices and had got themselves into a pickle weren't calling us for help and advice, they were calling us so they could just dump their animals and run. We were fast becoming the one-stop shop for owners looking for an easy way out.

The sanctuary was certainly saving lives but I was feeling more and more troubled that we weren't breaking the cycle, and in that respect we were failing the animals. We weren't being allowed, or maybe we weren't taking the opportunity, to teach the owners responsibility. As usual, I pondered on it for a while. Jim and I agreed that we weren't prepared to give up, we just needed to be a little smarter.

I do my best thinking in the shower and one particular morning as I was waiting for the conditioner to condition I was tossing around the idea of rebranding the sanctuary. I thought about giving it a name that told people we were there to help, but that they must play a role in their animals' futures too. Whether we were being asked for help or to take a pet, I wanted our name to suggest that the owner was part of the solution. I pondered extracting the word 'kura' out of Pakuratahi, the name of the area we live in. Kura means 'to educate or to teach' in Maori, but I wanted something a little less obvious than the obvious. I also knew I would have to get iwi—Maori tribe—permission and I didn't feel it would be likely for such a strong and important word. So as the conditioner conditioned I started throwing together letters and forming acronyms . . . And there it was, obvious and yet not obvious: HUHA—Helping You Help Animals. Our first point of contact, our brand was saying that 'we are here to help you' and it was the emphasis on the 'you' that gave us hope. So the trademark paperwork was submitted and we began our new journey, with the confidence that with a name like HUHA we could change attitudes and expectations in the community.

Back at my desk at the SPCA, I had just put down the receiver after talking to a woman about her son's dog. Her son had jetted off on his Overseas Experience and left his mother in sole charge of his dog. He, like many adolescent pet owners, hadn't taken full responsibility for finding a suitable solution for his dog when his life changed; he had just left his mother to pick up the pieces. We often say that a pet is not an Xbox, and so many young folk who love the idea of a cool companion to play with don't realise the gravity of the commitment. They can't just chuck their pet in the cupboard or walk away when they have had enough . . . and yet sadly so often they do! Understandably, the unprepared mother wasn't coping as she was working full-time and to top it off she was a little scared of the big mastiff–Staffy cross. She explained that he had been raised with small children, cats and a bunny rabbit. His bed was a beanbag in their lounge.

'Can you please take him? I just can't do this any more,' she sobbed down the phone.

I actually did have one spare kennel, so if he fitted the shelter criteria I might just be able to help, and to be honest I was sick to death of constantly turning folk away. With the capacity to hold only twelve dogs, including the seized dogs, and such tough criteria set by the powers-that-be, I found myself in the awful position of saying no more than yes. This was not my style at all. I always tried to offer helpful suggestions and alternative solutions, but often we were the public's last call before the final visit to the vet.

'Bring him down this afternoon and if he fits the criteria then of course we will help,' I reassured her. My fingers were crossed as I hung up the phone.

A few hours later I met the lady and her dog in the car park. My heart sank. With his muscular build, light piercing eyes and red nose, he was most certainly of pitbull heritage.

The woman stood anxiously with the big lug of a dog sitting nicely next to her.

'Can you tell me again what breed he is?' I asked.

She could see the disappointment in my eyes and replied, 'My son told me to say he was a mastiff cross.' She looked as defeated as I felt.

He actually looked like a lovely dog, and as I offered him my hand to sniff he happily allowed me to tickle him under the chin. His tail wagged enthusiastically as he repositioned himself and leaned into my leg. He was just a big goof. But with his light eyes and red nose, he would be a dead goof if I allowed him to place one foot inside the shelter. There was absolutely no denying that he was a pitbull and that was a breed the SPCA did not entertain.

To be fair, pitbulls are very hard to place. They often have had such a rough upbringing that they come with a lot of emotional baggage. Combine that with an innate nature to guard and protect and sometimes that baggage presents itself in the form of aggression. An unhappy or insecure pitbull can be a very tricky dog to work with, let alone rehome. Although I often had pitbulls in my care at the shelter, awaiting processing by the inspectors, I had never been allowed the opportunity to take one through a training or rehabilitation programme. There was no movement on that rule and even the sweetest natured and wiggly bottomed puppies, as I suspected this big boy once was, were destroyed. No discussion or correspondence would be entered into on this firmly entrenched rule.

I stood quietly with this beautiful dog still happily leaning up against me. I hate to feel defeated. This lady had had to face the reality of working full-time and not being strong enough to walk him; I could have worked her through those issues and made valid and helpful suggestions but the overriding fact was that she didn't want the dog and the daily responsibility to care for him was too much.

Then all at once I remembered a friend of a friend whose old Staffy-pitbull cross had just died at the impressive age of fifteen years. I asked the lady to wait in the car park as I ran inside and made a few phone calls. After ringing around I found this guy and, yes, if it was the right dog he was nearly ready to love again.

As the 34-year-old self-employed tradesman walked down the driveway towards us, the big blobby pitbull noticed him right away. His excited tail wag graduated to a full-blown bottom wag. He reared with delight on the end of the lead as he realised that the young man was actually coming straight for him. I couldn't help but tear up as the man dropped to his knees and wrapped his arms around the big boy. It was as if no one else existed.

Both of us in tears, the lady and I hugged each other, and hugged the tradie. Her son's dog was not going to die that day but instead he would gain a new master. A kind, caring and responsible master who would protect him and keep him out of harm's way in such a judgemental world.

CHAPTER 16

The neighbours

The saying goes that 'you can choose your friends but you can't pick your family'.

Jim and I both have the most wonderful supportive families so that doesn't resonate with us, but if you put a twist on the saying, to 'you can choose your friends but you can't pick your neighbours' then, boom, there it was, the bane of our otherwise very happy lives.

'It only takes one bad apple to spoil the bunch' is another saying that aptly described our reality. Jim and I kept to ourselves, we worked hard and tried to do this as selflessly as possible. Maybe it's true that people are afraid of what they don't understand, and for whatever reason one set of neighbours on our shared Kaitoke driveway hated us.

Hate is a pretty strong word, but as the years have gone by, yip, hate is pretty accurate. The story started off badly enough but it got dramatically worse. In fact, fast forward fourteen years to just a few weeks ago and you will see seven armed officers, pretty much the entire Upper Hutt police force, with rifles and tasers, asking our neighbour to come out of his house with his hands up, then to take his shirt off and lie face down on the ground. All because of his undying fixation on and resentment towards us.

Now let's rewind back to the beginning and look at the basic facts. It was silly of us to buy on a shared driveway and we have to take responsibility for that. And maybe our original plans to save the animal world were a little ambitious for some locals to understand or cope with. But, having said that, the difficult neighbours had not yet built a house on their plot of land up the shared driveway and our other two neighbours who also share the driveway are warm and caring folk. They often say that having a sanctuary close by is something that delights them. But the bad apples did build a home below our little hill, and it seemed that the bigger we grew and the more support we attracted, the nastier and more destructive they became. We just completely underestimated how nasty they would be.

It's an awful feeling to be under attack. It's an even worse feeling when you just can't understand why.

My very wise mum said to me as I was rocking in a corner one day, 'There are people in the world who see things very black and white. To them, they are either winning or they are losing. And when these folk see you win, they assume that that means they are losing, so they armour up and start to attack.'

Our very scary neighbours had become more agitated with us and I just couldn't understand why. If we were to pinpoint the exact moment they turned feral on us it would be the time we gave their son an old car. It had been sitting parked and unused on our driveway for a while, so when their son was released from prison and they sent him to ask us if he could have it, we said yes. We knew he was looking for work and commended his attitude. The deal was that he could have the car if he helped us pick up some fresh cut hay from the paddock, which he did. It was the weekend and we also said it would pay not to drive the car until the ownership papers were submitted, which he didn't . . . didn't listen or didn't care, we are not sure which.

Then a few hundred dollars worth of speeding and parking tickets promptly arrived in our postbox addressed to me. I wasn't too worried about the tickets as it was clearly just a muddle up, and we popped down the hill to pass them over to our neighbours. And that's when it happened. Apparently it was our fault for giving their son the car and if we were gullible enough to give it away then the tickets were our problem. We clearly weren't going to get anywhere with the neighbours, so I rang the enforcement agencies and had the tickets transferred into their name and we went about our business.

While we were getting on with our lives it would seem they were getting on with campaigning to get rid of us from the neighbourhood. Geese by the river a kilometre away, lambs popping through farm fencing, bulls running up the road, cows and horses on the state highway, seagulls in the sky, nomadic peacocks passing through the valley—it didn't matter that none of these animals were ours nor that we weren't involved in these situations at all, we always seemed to get the blame. We did our best to ignore the gossip and just got on with what we were doing.

But that wasn't the end of it.

CHAPTER 17

Libby and co.

I love chooks. There is something truly delightful and comical about them.

My mother always said she loved how they hitched their britches up as they ran for their breakfast.

So when the production team for the *Lord of the Rings* called and asked if we could help out with some Hobbiton pick-ups, we were especially excited to hear they needed chickens, along with a goat and some sheep. Pick-ups are, as their name suggests, when the director goes back and picks up little bits and pieces of footage that may have been missed, overlooked or just didn't work the first time round when filming. So with three of the pre-trained motley crew and some feathered-up and perky ex-battery hens on board we drove into the city to Peter Jackson's studio.

When *LOTR* had begun production, I was still busy in my own world of training animals on the set of the children's TV series. It wasn't until a few years later that I was looking for more work. A friend of mine who was an assistant manager in the extras' wardrobe department hired me as a on-set wardrobe assistant, so instead of wrangling animals I found myself wrangling sandals and boots and the blood-stained dirty rags that we carefully draped and tied around the orcs. It was so much fun dressing the orcs and attentively following them on set to keep them cool under the harsh summer sun. The job was very serious and rewarding, and as we moved around the different locations and worked on making all the different extra characters comfortable, my mind boggled at what a complete monster the *LOTR* beast was! As the Ringwraith riders galloped past, doing their seemingly dangerous and impossible stunts, I was secretly pleased that I wasn't involved in the animal side of things.

Watching the chaos during the shooting and hearing the behind-the-scenes gossip was an eye and ear opener. As far as I could see, everything was kept as safe and as professional as possible, and the animals had undergone months of specialist training and were completely prepared for their roles. But some of the war scenes—with the pure adrenaline, the crashing and bashing, the pushing and shoving, and the whites of the horses' eyes as they tossed their heads—looked a little too full-on for my comfort. This movie and its animal department was way out of my league.

But I'm not someone who can walk away from what I see in front of me, and I decided that I needed to know the facts. So I hunted down the animal welfare representatives, the people who make sure that everything is kosher and allow the 'no animals were harmed in the making of this movie' disclaimer to be displayed in the credits. They were great, well trained and very serious about their duties, though I wondered how they coped with the pressure. I certainly didn't envy them during the violent simulated fight scenes, but they were confident that everything was acceptable and assured me that they spoke out if they were ever worried.

After my stint in wardrobe I decided to take a break and

put myself through the Animal Welfare Inspectors course, the same one that qualifies the SPCA inspectors. I flew to and from Auckland three times to sit and learn. Animal welfare was essentially what made the blood pump through my veins and I nailed the course and was a star student. But in true dyslexic style, I never quite got around to handing in all of my homework.

About a month after the course had finished, I was called on to be one of the on-set welfare representatives for *LOTR*. The scene I was observing involved just the one horse. The character Aragon had been washed up on a river's edge, and a horse called Brego finds the exhausted warrior and nudges him awake. The horse then lays down so that Aragon can drag himself onto its back and the two quietly amble away. Thank goodness it wasn't a war scene; I quite possibly would have been a complete wreck.

As I finished inspecting the sand that the horse was to lay on, checking for rocks or any other uncomfortable or dangerous debris, I gave the first assistant director the nod. Everything seemed good to go and he had my approval. I sat in the long grass behind the cameras with the vet and we watched the scene smoothly play out in front of us. The trainer had been flown in from Australia and he certainly knew his job well. There was a sense of calm and the horse was well rehearsed and at peace with the action required. It was a good day.

But back to the pick-ups. Jim and I arrived at the studio with the ex-battery girls, Thistle the goat, Ernie the sheep and Arnold, another very special sheep I had hand-raised from an unwanted triplet lamb into a large, handsome and very social fellow.

We were shown by the director exactly what he needed from us. Ernie, Arnold and Thistle were essentially just very good-looking props, with the easy job of hanging with the hobbits in the background of the shot. But the chook action was going to be much more fun. They were front and centre with the main character of the scene and the director was after some pretty particular A to Bs.

'Are you sure the chickens will do that?' the assistant director, or AD, quietly asked us when the director was out of earshot. 'There is no time to muck around here. Time is money.'

I looked at Jim and we both nodded.

Usually we would have had prep time to teach an action prior to filming, but because we were pulled in last minute and the person who had hired us didn't have any idea what would be involved with the scene, we were just grateful to have our trusted motley crew, and beloved and thankfully clicker-trained chooks on hand.

Jim and I had both nursed Libby the battery hen back to life after we had rescued her and 24 others during our very first battery hen liberation. She had arrived at HUHA collapsed and weak. But as she regained her strength she blossomed into a hugely confident and forthright character. We named her Libby (short for liberation) and enjoyed her antics so much that we would never underestimate the wonder of a chicken again. Libby enjoyed being part of the action, any action. If something was going on then there she was right in the middle of it. Being such a smart cookie we decided it would be a fun project to clicker train her and she was a pro in just a few short sessions. But while Libby certainly stood out from the crowd, her feathered friends were no shrinking violets either and enjoyed the fun and games too. In fact, even today, after rescuing, rehabilitating and rehoming thousands and thousands of ex-commercial chooks they just never cease to amaze and delight us.

The scene was to be filmed on an elevated stage, about ten square metres and in front of a giant green screen. The chooks' job was to enter from stage right, walk to the hobbit in the centre of the stage, stand with him for ten seconds or so, follow him as he moved around the stage, and then, at the director's nod, he wanted the chooks to exit stage left.

Jim, clicker in hand, was poised and ready at stage left. We had already run Libby and her team of seven lady friends through their passes as a warm-up. When we were asked if they would like to rehearse with the talent we said no thank you. In situations like this it's often the first take that's the best, and we didn't want the girls to lose their edge. We had sprinkled the centre stage mark with just enough grain to get the girls to pause at the hobbit's feet and we had given the hobbit just enough grain to sprinkle as he walked around. Jim had the big guns, though: the clicker that, once clicked, triggered the girls to strut at a firm pace towards it.

'Aaaaand action,' the AD called.

Everything went quiet. All eyes were on us. I quickly kissed the girls on the forehead for luck and placed them at stage right. One by one they did their little Cleopatra walk to the centre of the stage where they hovered around the hobbit's feet, pecking at the grain. As the hobbit moved to the back of the stage the girls happily followed seeing the light sprinkle of food falling from his pocket. Then with one click from stage left their beautiful heads turned and one by one they did their little Cleopatra walk off towards the edge of stage left.

'Still rolling,' hollered the AD as he bent to listen to the director's instructions.

The hobbits were still acting beautifully, quietly going through the motions of smiling and nodding between themselves, interacting with and patting Arnold, Thistle and Ernie as they were slowly being led around as background action.

As the AD stood up straight he called, 'And still rolling, can we have some more farmyard movement and if the chickens could walk back over to stage right, stopping at the hobbit for a few moments on the way.'

'Oh crikey, where's my clicker,' I mumbled to myself.

Jim had just released the girls again and they were making their way back to the hobbit with perfect poise and style. They checked him out for a few seconds then started to look as if they might scatter off in different directions. Just at that moment I laid my desperately searching hand on a clicker in pocket number four of my cargo pants. I let out a click and the girls perked up their heads, turned and started to methodically walk to stage right. Phew! They were absolute stars.

'And it's a wrap. Thank you.' The AD smiled at us and said, 'They are very impressive chickens, who knew?'

Tee hee, I thought to myself . . . we knew.

CHAPTER 18

A wanted dog

Even at 22 years old Shaun still has a scar on his face where Murphy bit him.

I will never forgive myself for putting either of them in that situation, but it gave me a much better understanding of what it means to keep your pets safe.

Our big boy Murphy was now ten years old and had been suffering from joint pain for some time. We had him on various meds and potions, but he was sore and he was getting more and more cranky, and as a result he had started to guard himself. Shaun, now around twelve, was having a sleepover at our house with the young boys who lived on the farm next door. I seriously don't know what I was thinking, or maybe I wasn't thinking, as the boys, and Murphy, all headed into Shaun's bedroom and into their sleeping bags.

It was another hour or so before Shaun came running out of his room with blood streaming down his face, his voice hoarse from screaming as he announced that Murphy had bitten him. We were all in tears in a matter of minutes and his friends were shuttled out the door back home. We were clueless as to what to do next. With pressure applied to his face, Shaun was bundled into the car. And with more pain meds on board, Murph was placed on the back seat next to him. Murphy was far from a vicious attacker, and had essentially been bombproof since he'd come to live with us.

The scenario probably went something like this: as the boys had started to quieten down the dozing Murphy had most likely fallen into a deep sleep. When Shaun had leant down to give his buddy a kiss goodnight, Murphy had woken with a start and bitten Shaun's face. We wondered if maybe Shaun had leaned on Murph's leg or somehow triggered some pain, because our gentle old boy loved Shaun and would never intentionally hurt him.

Oh hell, what to do next? We had never been in a situation like this.

As the doctor stitched Shaun's cheek, he questioned Jim and me about what had happened. 'I'm going to have to report this, you know. It could have been extremely serious; if the bite had been a few centimetres higher it could have been the lad's eye.'

We sat numbly with our heads hung low. Oh God, we were thinking, we are terrible parents. Not just to Shaun, but to Murphy too. Why oh why didn't we protect them both? We thought it was cute that the boys had wanted Murphy to be part of their sleepover but things were definitely far from cute now.

'So you will be euthanising the dog, correct?' the doctor continued.

Oh, how I just wanted to be back on my bus, far away from all the pressure and responsibility. The doctor took our details and said the authorities would be notified. Thank goodness Shaun would be just fine, but all we could think about was the damage control needed for such a highly reactive situation. Shaun's mother was, as expected, a mixture of upset and angry, and we knew in the cold light of day that the authorities could be coming for our big boy.

Murphy had not aged well. His giant bones had not been nurtured at the all-important growth stage and he was now suffering for it. Sometimes he bounced around pain-free, but then there were times that the meds just didn't seem to work. The week before, he had bitten a baby goat that was skipping past him and had hopped too close to his legs. The signs were there that Murphy was struggling, and although he had been given all the vet care we could offer, we had to admit we had the blinkers on as to how serious his situation was becoming. Our predicament was just horrible, and we were not experienced enough to know what to do.

From my work at the SPCA I knew by their standards that Murph was not a good homing option. As a vet nurse I knew he was already on the best pain meds. As a step-mum I knew that the kids loved Murphy more than words could say but that their mother would not let this go. I also knew it was my fault, that I had been too cavalier and hadn't protected my family. I was a responsible member of society and I knew that Murphy's actions would not be tolerated, that he was about to become a wanted dog.

So we rang a vet who I worked closely with and he agreed to open the clinic for us. It had been such an alarming and unexpected night, and as we cuddled and held Murphy I knew that I was never ever going to forgive myself. He slipped into a deep sleep and I bent down and kissed my big friend on the cheek for the last time.

I can't describe how terrible it all was. Things felt so hurried and so forced, but there was no way we would let the authorities take Murph away only to reach the same decision. Murphy was one of the great loves of our lives and we wanted to be the ones to hold him when he went. It may not have been on our terms, but at least we still had some sort of control.

Years later I am still haunted by Murphy's death. But what is the point of living through such a great loss if I didn't learn anything? I could put my guilt at ease and say it was the arthritis in his old age that killed our big boy. But that would not be true. The lesson I have taken from this situation is that it was my responsibility as a parent to supervise my children with my dog. Children should never ever be left alone with dogs, whether a puppy or an adult. It was my job to protect both Shaun and Murphy, and I failed on both counts.

At HUHA today we have many dogs that come through the system with both old and new injuries and conditions. Our team, who you will meet a bit later, always remembers my story of Murphy, and how he died that night. The animals that need special care we carefully rehome with adults who have no children or who have grown-up children. We explain to owners that if they have a busy day of visitors then to just pop the dog away from it all. We explain it is their responsibility not to put anyone, dog included, in a silly situation. And above all never ever leave children alone with dogs.

Murphy's ashes sit in our family room next to those of Haggis and Gerber, who both passed peacefully and surrounded with love.

CHAPTER 19

A change of environment

As Jim and I struggled through the ups and downs of rescue work we noticed that every bad situation always had a silver lining.

Whether it be a lesson learnt or new relationship built, there was always something. And with Pixie the pony we gained both.

The lesson we learnt was that it is not always possible to get it right. No matter how careful we were when choosing a new home and no matter how good the new owners seemed at the time, situations and even agendas can change. The most important thing then is for us to stay available and be there if we are ever needed to pick up the pieces.

I remember like it was yesterday the day Pixie's owner called us.

'If you don't come and get this bloody pony, I'm gonna lose it. I'm gonna give her the bash,' said the voice down the other end of the phone.

Slightly alarmed by the threat, I talked more with Pixie's mum, methodically retrieving information so I could piece together the scenario that had led to her making the phone call.

'So are you saying you want to hit your pony?' I carefully asked in a pleasant tone.

'Yeah, nah, it's bloody driving me around the bend. The cheeky tart's pushing all my buttons and, honestly, I don't damn well trust myself with her . . . can you take her or not?'

What a character. They were big fighting words, but under all the bravado I could hear in her voice that despite the meltdown she cared deeply for the pony and its future. As we talked further she explained in her clumsy way that she didn't want Pixie going just anywhere. She told me that she was a very experienced horsewoman and if she couldn't cope with the brat of a pony then she worried no one else would be able to. She just wanted Pixie safe and out of harm's way . . . hers was essentially an honest cry for help.

As I hung up the phone and relayed the content of the call to Jim, I added, 'If only more folk were brave enough to ask for an intervention.'

Within the hour we were at her house and Pixie was introducing herself to Jim and me. She was stunning, a steel grey pure-bred Welsh mountain pony, only two years old. Her owner was right, she was a hugely extroverted character and with both of them having opinionated and bolshy natures it was very apparent why they clashed.

She explained that when Pixie was just days old her mother died after eating something poisonous and that Pixie had to be bottle-fed by her breeder. The lady had bought Pixie off the breeder just six months ago, and she had already broken her to saddle.

We said our goodbyes and took Pixie home where she took a shine to the motley crew straight away. They kept her entertained and out of mischief, enjoying her cheeky games, and leaving her happy and satisfied. With all her new friends Pixie settled quickly and was a complete angel.

As we often say, change the environment and you will change the animal, and for Pixie this is exactly what happened. She was just a baby, and didn't want to work and be pressured. She wanted to enjoy her childhood and frolic, and the sanctuary's hills and gullies were just the magical playground in which she could thrive for the next few years.

As she grew we discovered that she loved to ride in horse floats and hopped aboard for an outing at any opportunity. She also loved to be brushed and cuddled by Leah and any visitor she could work her magic on.

Not wanting to become hoarders, and always needing space for new rescues, we look for a caring new home to place an animal in after rehabilitation. We are very careful to choose homes that continue to provide a fun and enriched environment where the new family member will be loved for life. And we are usually very careful to find a home where the animal won't be bred (there are enough to rescue without creating more!). And that's where I mucked up with Pixie. My judgement became clouded and I was about to make a humungous and devastating mistake.

A woman came to visit us at the sanctuary, and wanted to take Pixie. She had other Welsh mountain ponies for her to play with and was keen to take Pixie to shows. As Pixie loved to ride in the float and loved to play and show off and be groomed and fluffed over, it seemed a perfect match—though we were very sad to see her go!

The first time we visited Pixie everything seemed fine; she was her usual happy-go-lucky self. Sometime later we visited her again and she had a beautiful newborn foal at her feet. Pixie and the foal looked happy and healthy. But we told the lady that we weren't keen on Pixie becoming a brood mare and because she had not been taken out for adventures, but left in a small and boring paddock to breed, we would be taking Pixie back once their prize foal was weaned.

Several months later we went to collect Pixie. Our hearts sank. She was shockingly skinny and very depressed—her foal had been weaned and Pixie had been left on her own in an even smaller paddock. I was inconsolable. I had failed little Pixie. The light had gone out of her eyes, and when we rolled back her lips to check her teeth, we could see immediately that her front teeth were severely worn from grazing the sparse and stony paddock she had been left in. We took Pixie home with us and set about loving her back to wellness. But Pixie found it hard to cheer up and her weight loss remained a problem. We cried and felt terrible that we had ever let her go!

One day we saw Pixie's foal 'Fern' advertised for sale on the internet. We drove to the property and banged on the door. To this day I don't think I have ever lost my temper and yelled the way I did at those people.

'You put Pixie through all this to get a foal and now you are throwing that away too? No way, that's not good enough. That foal does not deserve to be sold like a second-hand toy. How dare you!'

After my enraged outburst they agreed that we could take the foal away then and there. I took a deep breath and refocused. As we calmly and gently approached Fern her eyes widened with panic, and she thrashed around the pen. It was clear she had had very little or no handling. But with patience and kindness we managed to get a halter on her and brought her home.

We watched the emotional reunion. Delighted to see her

mum, Fern nuzzled and mouthed at Pixie in the submissive way foals often do, then, as she gained her confidence, soon became playful and animated. Fern was definitely scared of people and a little thin but otherwise okay. And, oh, how we hoped that she would help heal Pixie's broken spirit and broken heart.

Several months later Pixie had finally started to fill out and look her healthy beautiful self once again. Then one morning, as we were wandering through the paddock, we noticed something moving on the ground by Pixie's feet. As we edged forward for a closer look, to our amazement and complete horror we found Pixie was standing next to a newborn foal. Once again, I felt the guilt take over as I sat on the ground and sobbed. Pixie was looking amazing; she was truly almost back to her old self—and we were delighted to meet little Punga, we truly were. But it was just so devastating to think that Pixie would have been pregnant with him all the time she was depressed and emaciated.

So while trying to rehome one pony we somehow ended up with three!

As we watched cheeky Punga grow and constantly hassle his mother and sister to play, the horror of Pixie's journey started to fade in our minds and we hoped in hers too.

'So how do we go about rehoming them now?' I asked Jim, knowing that we had become so very attached to and protective of Pixie and her little family.

'We don't,' he said with conviction.

I looked into his eyes to try to gauge if he was serious. And he was.

So we have kept Pixie, Fern and Punga together here at the sanctuary. And they have a very important job of interacting with visiting children as part of our educational programme. We even use them to help at-risk youth process their emotions through our Equine Growth and Learning Programme.

But every sunrise, as I watch our terrific trio galloping across the hills in pursuit of Jim on his quad bike, I am reminded just how lucky we are to have had a second chance. We truly are on such a huge journey when it comes to learning about people and animals, and it just goes to show that we can never take our role and our choices for granted, no matter how careful and experienced we think we are at choosing new homes. Things can sometimes go wrong, whether it be a change in circumstances or misjudging someone's intentions, or maybe a lapse of judgement with a new owner. We are so invested in every single animal that leaves our care and promise that we will always be available should any of them need us for any reason in the future.

We are just so grateful that with Pixie and her little family we were in a position to put things right.

CHAPTER 20

King Kong and some monkeys

Jim and I were chuffed to be asked to head the animal department for Peter Jackson's movie *King Kong*.

And we were even more excited when we saw the haphazard collection of animals we would need to provide and train. Well, all except for one.

On the list was a mynah bird for the ship's galley, a cart horse, and several police horses for the New York City streets, a parrot and a marauding dog. The one we weren't excited about was a monkey riding a bicycle, which was obviously not an enjoyable natural behaviour for a monkey and against our moral beliefs. After carefully voicing our concern and trying to think of alternatives, we were so relieved when we were told the monkey had been just a vague idea the art department had for one of the early vaudeville theatre scenes, which probably wouldn't happen anyway.

The sad thing is that we actually thought we might know where we could get a monkey riding a bicycle, or riding a pony at the very least, and the more we thought about the heinous idea, the more curious we became. So, armed with a good excuse to have a sneaky peek behind the scenes, we took the opportunity to have our first up-close-and-personal experience with the ringmaster of a little New Zealand travelling circus. We correctly introduced ourselves as animal trainers and casting agents and the ringmaster happily showed us around. Stepping back in time and walking past the chained elephant, the tethered donkeys and the tied-up mutant dwarf pony, Jim and I both started to feel uncomfortable. As the ringmaster proudly introduced us to the lions in a makeshift enclosure, I thought inwardly that the male, supposedly the most majestic creature in the world, had such sadness about him and literally no mane, just a scruffy effort that truly didn't count.

We approached the monkeys who, like most of the animals, were on chains and tethers. We met three of them: Laurie a 'badly behaved' capuchin and the new up-and-coming stars, pig-tailed macaque sisters Joanna and Rachel. Rachel and Joanna had ropes bolted around their necks and were also inside one of the portable chainlink enclosures. Apparently they were only young, just two years old, and the ringmaster was still working on breaking their spirits so they would work well for him and ride the pony. As we made our excuses to leave, the ringmaster pointed inside the tent. There was one more monkey to see. His old boy Charlie, a rhesus macaque, liked to hide out away from prying eyes, and as our eyes pried our hearts sank. Charlie was clearly very old; he was hunched and his limbs noticeably twisted with arthritis. He was sitting quietly on a bench seat under the dark red glow of the unlit tent. It was obvious he just wanted to be left alone, so we snuck out as quickly and quietly as we snuck in. We had had our first look at the reality of a cruel and antiquated part of

New Zealand history. We sat in sombre silence all the way home.

The rest of the animals for *King Kong* were easily cast and played their parts well. The endless supply of money was a mystery to us and extremely hard to get used to. We flew our star mynah bird Birdy Num Nums down from Auckland to merely sit as a prop bird in a cage in the ship's galley. When the scenes wrapped, we flew him home. Just a month later he was needed again, so the jet-setting bird was put on a plane and flown back down to Wellington, then back to Auckland, then he was needed *again* and flew down one more time. This to-ing and fro-ing seemed to be the nature of the film.

We spent hours casting and preparing the mounted police, both the riders and the horses, for the city of New York scenes. We rode the horses through the city set, desensitising them by getting them used to every aspect of the amazingly detailed city that had been recreated in an old industrial lot in Seaview. But after the crowd scenes were shot, all footage of the mounted police landed on the cutting room floor. Tens of thousands of dollars, and time and effort, were gone, just like that. It wasn't something to dwell on though; throwing away footage was commonplace, and something I imagined everyone else working so tirelessly on the film had to come to terms with. The director had his vision and the finished product was all that counted.

One animal that did get a surprisingly large cameo in the final cut was our beloved Ned. We cast him to be a marauding street dog in the slums of New York, right at the beginning of the film. Blink and you'll miss him, but as far as extras go on a huge budget movie like this, his was a bit of a coup. His little deformed leg made him the perfect tragic scrounger. He looked a little too Australian, so out with the non-toxic black face paint and hair gel, and soon Ned was in character and looking every bit the dirty and desperate New York hobo. The director loved him and asked for one camera to stay just on him throughout the takes. So with Jim and me hiding strategically behind the ramshackle huts, tossing morsels of food among the litter as take after take was filmed, Ned worked his magic and stole the hearts of everyone on set that day.

CHAPTER 21

A devastating journey

Back in the real world I signed up for another locum nursing job, this time at a Wellington vet clinic that had just opened its doors and was not yet fully staffed.

It was a small clinic and an hour's drive away but the part-time hours suited me. I could care for and feed all the sanctuary animals in the morning and then leave for the clinic at lunchtime. As the weeks turned into months my locum position merged into something a little more permanent. Well, at least for a few years.

It was about 7 p.m. and Alastair, the resident vet and clinic owner, and I were about to head to our respective homes for the night. I was so absorbed in mopping the floor after the last rather smelly consult for the evening that I hadn't got around to switching the phone over to the after-hours emergency message. Alastair was trying to balance my slightly-out-of-whack till takings. The frustrating thing is that the till just never balanced on my shifts, so instead of racing out the door and leaving me to it, Alastair had learnt the drill and would patiently wait for the inevitable cry for help. So as his dinner grew colder at home he would sit wearing a face that resembled Jim's during his morning Sudoku routine, and work his way through the ledger and receipts. As I put the mop away and walked over to the phone, it started to ring. The caller explained that there was an emergency on one of the freight ferries. He asked if we could please come to the dock at speed. There were nine dogs in a very serious state, with some already dead.

As we threw the emergency kit in the back of my new old 4x4 people mover I explained to Alastair that the caller had said the dogs had overheated in a vehicle. We loaded up with drip lines, fluids and ice packs and sped down the hill. When we approached the wharf there were very sombre-looking men waving their arms and guiding us towards the back of the freight ferry. We drove up the ramps into the dimly lit hull. It was like a ghost town, no other people or vehicles in sight. We drove up one more ramp to the next parking level and stared in disbelief at what lay before us. There on the cold metal floor were what looked like nine dead bodies, all lined up in a row. I grabbed the stethoscope and threw it to Alastair who started to assess each lifeless body, one after another. As he quickly made his way along the line, he'd pause briefly before moving to the next dog, looking up at their expectant guardian and remorsefully shaking his head. I had been working my way back from the other end of the queue, looking for a breath, feeling for a heartbeat, desperate for any sign of life. And then we saw a dog in the centre of the line-up give the tiniest gasp.

He was alive! And to our surprise and relief the dog next in line did the same.

Only two survivors. Our hearts were aching.

But we threw everything we had into the frail older hunt-away and his younger heading dog friend. Alastair managed to insert a catheter into each dog's fragile vein with expert precision. As the fluid pumped through their exhausted and dehydrated bodies the young heading dog started to bounce back. The old boy took a lot longer to rally, but eventually his breathing became more deliberate and his heart rate stronger. We had surrounded them with ice packs to help get their temperature down, but it was a fine line and as we monitored them the ice packs were ditched and they were snuggled in blankets.

While I sat with the two dogs in the back of my 4x4, Alastair took a moment to talk to his guardian. He was a young farmer, no more than twenty years old, and he and a team of cockies and their dogs had been working a farm in the deep south. That job was finished and they were relocating to the lower North Island to start another big muster. The lad had a pretty nice ute. Instead of a canopy over the tray it had one of those flat tops that have a 20-centimetre gap running around the circumference for air flow. It would have been okay I guess to transport a dog or two back there, but the young fellow had jammed nine excited farm dogs into the tray before setting off on a ten-hour journey. Overcrowded was an understatement! And when the ute parked up in the hull of the container ship, the air had stopped flowing and the dogs were overcome by heat exhaustion.

It was a devastating error in judgement. Seven hard-working loyal dogs were dead. I hated to think how he was going to tell the other farmers that their valued companions and tools of their trade hadn't made it. The young farmer was sobbing, and looked in complete shock. As I stared up into his eyes they looked tortured; it was clear this was something he was never going to get over.

As we drove the two survivors back to the clinic for a night of rest and fluids I asked Alastair if he'd like me to call my friends at the SPCA.

'No,' he said quietly, 'that young boy has already paid the price for his actions.'

CHAPTER 22

Gut instinct

Well, hooray for gut instincts! So often we get them, but I was constantly left wondering whether these unsubstantiated feelings should be embraced or ignored.

Though as the years have passed, I would have to note that nine out of ten times our gut instincts are bang on.

On one occasion I got myself in a little trouble with my gut instinct.

On paper the Smiths were perfect: animal mad with lots of love and land on offer and to top it off nicely the wife was a vegetarian! No better home could be expected for our pets-only forever-home criteria; at HUHA our animals for rehoming are not for killing, eating or breeding. Except there was that niggling gut feeling.

When I phoned them to say that we wouldn't be giving any of HUHA's sanctuary pigs or cows to them for adoption, but we wished them well, there were tears, tantrums and a late-night abusive phone call. As I arrived at my part-time job at the Wellington vet clinic, I was sat down and told that the Smiths, who happened to be clients of the clinic, were so offended by my actions that they and their extended family were boycotting the clinic while I was still in its employ! Thank goodness my boss valued me and my job was safe, but my gut instincts had landed me in more than a little trouble that day and I was left wondering if I was right. The thought did briefly cross my mind that maybe I was over-analysing the situation and perhaps I was just a judgemental meanie!

I had accepted that I'd never know if my intuition was right or if I was way out of line, when several months later Jim wandered into the lounge one afternoon, grinning at me.

'There you go, you can put yourself out of your misery.' As he tossed me the paper he exclaimed, 'You were right!'

As I started to read the article headed 'These little piggies have roast beef', my jaw dropped. The sweet animal-hugging vegetarian, who had condemned me so harshly for not adopting out our animals to her, had started a free-range home-kill meat business and breeding facility. There she was with her husband, proudly cuddling one of their pigs. The article went into detail about how much they loved their lifestyle, their animals and their new wonderful service to the community.

While I agree that free-range pig farming can be a momentous improvement on the cruel practice of factory farming, I think it's important for people to be honest and ethical in their intentions—a vegetarian pig farmer is somewhat hypocritical in my view!

'Hey Carolyn, I just drove past the circus and there were a whole lot of protesters picketing it.'

Jim was calling me from his cell phone. He made a great roving reporter, and could have had a job as the eye in the sky for the local radio station.

'Is it the elephant do you think?'

We had heard about the controversy surrounding this particular circus and its exploitation of exotic animals. A year had passed since our sneak peek behind the scenes of this very circus, and the animals we had seen had not stopped preying on our minds. As Jim continued to talk, all the unpleasant memories came flooding back.

'What do you think, should we protest with them?' Jim had pulled over to watch the chaos as the big top was being erected in a local park.

'I don't know. I wonder if anyone has actually just talked to him . . . maybe we should try?'

As we sat with the ringmaster, we just listened at first. It was obvious he still loved an audience and he loved to tell his story. His was a classic; he had joined the circus as a boy and 50-odd years later it was all he knew. We asked him what his plans were and he admitted that he was tired and would love to slow down as his health was deteriorating. 'But with the bloody protesters on his back' he was too proud and stubborn to make the move.

Over the next week Jim and I went to the river and foraged for willow branches for the elephant, loaded up Jim's ute and drove our offerings to the circus. We became familiar faces and the team of roadies were always grateful for our help. Before long we were able to talk to the ringmaster about retiring the animals. There was the elephant, the monkeys, the donkeys and pony as well as the lions, poodles and doves. He agreed it was time to let all of them go, except for the poodles and doves which were his wife's much-loved pets. After doing the sums and assessing our land we gave ourselves a reality check; lions and an elephant were probably too much for us to handle and after talking with the ringmaster we knew he had other good offers on the table from established wildlife sanctuaries. No one, however, wanted the monkeys.

There were no sensible solutions in the pipeline, so we decided we would put our hands up. We also agreed to take Pablo the pony and Jenny and Wee One the donkeys back to HUHA.

The day we were going to pick up the monkeys came along in a bit of a hurry. The ringmaster wasn't well and needed to move them on faster than agreed. It was winter and the tricky thing was that we didn't have anywhere to put them yet, let alone have an official sign-off from the Ministry of Agriculture and Fisheries (MAF). The ringmaster insisted that they needed to be gone immediately. He also insisted that we pay for the monkeys' caravan and temporary enclosure as part of the deal for which he would accept no less than $20,000. We tried to reason with him but his final words were always, 'Well you can bugger off then, and they can stay here.'

We didn't want to lose the opportunity to get them out of the circus. We knew there was an opportunity for the ringmaster to sell them to another circus, so we weighed up our options and organised a second mortgage on our house. Forty thousand dollars, half for the caravan and half to build a big new enclosure for the monkeys as soon as the ground firmed.

MAF were amazing. They, too, were keen to see the circus animals retired and so instead of coming down heavily on this very peculiar last-minute transaction, they set about issuing us a temporary circus animal layover permit. As long as the monkeys' caravan was behind a 1.8-metre perimeter fence and we adhered to all the rules we would be okay.

Jim and I drove for four hours to collect the monkeys. We walked across the field towards the big top and took a shortcut, bypassing the front entrance, hopping over the barrier rope, and headed straight to the monkeys' caravan.

There was a bone-chilling noise in the air that we immediately identified as monkey screams. We looked at each other and flew around the corner to see what was going on.

It was horrible. A circus roadie, who had his back to us and didn't realise we were there, continued on with his game. The stick he was carrying was solid enough not to break as he ran it back and forth along the wire mesh that the monkeys sat trapped behind, and thin and long enough to be able to poke through the bars at the hysterically screaming monkeys. Circus folk are like family to one another, and we knew that if we made a scene all deals would be off, so we dropped back and reapproached from the front in full view. By the time we were standing next to him the roadie's game was over and his stick had been replaced with a hose. He was giving the monkey caravan a final hose down for our benefit, and our hearts broke when we saw through the wire all three monkeys huddled in the back corner of their small compartments.

'Yeah, you only have to do this every few days,' the roadie announced in a helpful manner, a proud and slimy grin on his face.

'Don't you wait until they are out of their cages?' I asked with forced interest.

'Nah, they don't care,' he replied as he flicked icy water around in the wintry cold, wetting their bedding and ricocheting drops on the monkeys' quivering little bodies.

We couldn't get those little ones out of there fast enough. We handed over the money, loaded up our ute and attached the trailer containing three emotionally broken monkeys—Joanna had sadly died since our first visit—to the towbar, and we were gone. It was the second time we had driven away from the little circus quiet and sober. But this time we had made a difference; this time we had broken the cycle.

It's a weird feeling waking up to the realisation that there are monkeys in your garden. Having the monkeys at home gave me the sense that anything is achievable if you are driven, careful and strategic.

Although the three monkeys were now safe, for us and for them, the journey to find them happiness had only just begun. There were so many questions to answer. It was too wet and muddy underfoot to build the monkey facility, so how were we going to exercise them and keep them enriched over the winter months—especially if they had to stay in that awful prison of a caravan? How were we going to keep Charlie's crippled body as pain-free as possible? How were we going to handle tethering and walking monkeys on leads, which was so morally against every fibre of our beings? And how long was Laurie going to have to wear the soul-destroying chain that was bolted to his collar?

'This is just going to have to be a sticking-plaster period,' I said to Jim. 'We can't make it all perfect and undo all the damage with a magic wand. We will just have to suck it up and transition with them.'

I grimaced at the idea of a monkey on a tether and I hated them being trapped in that god-awful caravan. But from that point on we had to do everything properly and carefully for their sanity and safety, as well as ours. We would stick to the routine they knew for now.

One huge concern was how Rachel was coping without her sister. The transfer of the monkeys had happened in such a hurry we hadn't stopped to fully process the awful news that Joanna had died.

'We were so close to helping her,' Jim said, kicking at a rock on the driveway.

I could see the frustration on his face as he hung his head in grief and sorrow for a little monkey we barely knew. We had been told that while in the Hawke's Bay, Joanna had been tethered to a tree. The day was unprecedentedly hot, and when Joanna had knocked her water bowl over it hadn't taken long for the heat to consume her and she died of heatstroke in a matter of minutes. So just a month later, there we were, left with half of a duo. We couldn't even begin to understand what Rachel must be going through. So much change. So much devastation. Her life had been taken out of her control and now she had lost probably the only one who could truly comfort her.

Jim and I were wandering around The Warehouse like two new shell-shocked parents, picking out buckets, gloves and scrubbing brushes when I went off in the direction of the toy department. My lovely husband is amazing in so many ways, but he has zero tolerance for shopping, and as soon as I start to divert off the beaten track his lips begin to thin and his tone sharpens.

'Where are you going?' Jim called out.

'I think Rachel needs a toy,' I announced as I disappeared down the toy aisle.

Hmm, now which toy would I like if I were a lonely monkey? I wondered. I reappeared at Jim's side with a choice of three. A classic teddy, a little fluffy monkey and a soft Tigger rattle.

When we got home I couldn't wait to show Rachel the toys. First I offered up the little monkey, which she grabbed off me and immediately dropped. She displayed the same lack of interest in the teddy too. Then I passed her the Tigger rattle. Her eyes fixated on it as she carefully took it from my hand, and when she started to make kissy faces and coo softly to it we knew we had a winner. From then on there was never a moment that Rachel wasn't holding Tigger. We even bought her a second Tigger for emergencies and for switching when the original needed washing.

CHAPTER 23

Laurie

Jim had come up with a genius plan to build the three monkeys temporary bedrooms in one bay of our garage.

MAF approved the idea as an interim containment facility and we set to work straight away. Winter was getting wild and woolly and the cramped caravan just wasn't going to cut it.

Each of the monkeys had to be housed separately. There was no getting around it with their varying ages and species, as well as a whole lot of dysfunction. They liked to see each other but didn't want contact. The monkey garage was great. As the winds howled outside the monkeys were toasty warm under a heat lamp, with hammocks and interesting knobby tree trunks to climb and fresh leafy branches and ponga ferns brought in daily. They were as content as could be until we could build them their new enclosures.

When there were breaks in the weather we would clip an extra-long dog lead to each of their collars and take them for a stroll around the property, to climb a tree or be tethered to something fun and enriching. Laurie was the trickiest to convince to come out of his room. He still had the awful piece of chain bolted to his collar and he protected it like his life depended on it. We soon learnt to read how he was feeling and whether he wanted to engage with us or not by how he handled the chain. It was the only way he knew to communicate with us. We hated the chain but were glad it gave him the power of choice—something we assumed he had had little of.

On calm or sunny days we would hold up the clip of a lead and Laurie would react in one of two ways. The first way was to take the free end of the chain dangling from his neck and carefully pass the link through the mesh so we could attach the dog lead. We would then open his door and thread the lead right though. Laurie would jump up on a shoulder and we would head outside. He was just so nervous. Until he was safely up his favourite tree and making jungle noises, it was a matter of walking quietly and slowly so he wouldn't take fright and have a huge screaming meltdown.

The other reaction we would get was heartbreaking. He would hold the chain that dangled from his neck and cross both hands over it, shielding it against his chest. It was as if he was guarding it from us, protecting himself from his handler and whatever situation he was about to be forced into. He would scream and rock and chatter his teeth. In response, we would divert our eyes and just stand and breathe calmly until he settled, then offer him a positive experience, like passing him his favourite food, a grape.

Laurie's circus keepers had told us that he was no longer used in shows because he had become extremely unpredictable and would bite. Some of the acrobats in the circus had surreptitiously filmed footage of him being kept in a small dog crate away from the other animals. They were distressed by his level of care and leaked the sad footage to the media. So Jim continued to diligently sit with Laurie, and the more time they spent quietly and relaxed in each other's company the more familiar they became to each other. The two of them would spend hours just sitting with Laurie curled up on Jim's knee.

Together they were detoxing from the stresses of life.

Laurie's confidence just got better and better, and we discovered that he loved to 'paint'. When we first found him smearing his caravan with poo, we were saddened as we suspected it was a learned behaviour from the boredom of his captive life. But then we decided to evolve his passion into something a little healthier, and so with canvas, face paint and sponges placed in front of a very excited Laurie, he would, with the helpful assistance of Jim, paint. I loved to watch the two of them; they'd emerge from a session of great artistic focus both covered with paint from head to toe. Laurie didn't restrict himself just to paint and canvas; he helpfully redecorated his day hut too.

CHAPTER 24

Weathering the storms

It was one of those fluffy duvet mornings, when you are so warm and toasty in bed that you just can't help but wake up with a smile.

We hadn't slept through our alarm, which was a nice change, and Jim, followed by five dogs, had already found his way to the toilet and started on his Sudoku. I was contemplating my dash to the bathroom, but knew I could have another blissful twenty minutes if Jim's habits were true to form. The wind was lashing at the windows and in the dawn light I could make out the silhouettes of the young pine trees surrounding our house, bending as the strong gusts hit. I started to think about the day ahead: we had to check on the animals, make sure they were warm enough and unaffected by the storm. It was definitely a porridge-type of a morning for the monkeys.

And then we needed to get ready to go to court. Who knew a shared driveway could cause such drama?

The phone ringing next to the bed jolted me from my thoughts. It was my friend Sam doing her morning check-in. Sam is an amazingly kind and clever lady, and had become interested in HUHA work. When I first met her at the SPCA years earlier, her passion for horses and their rescue and rehabilitation brought us together. Aside from her regular visits to the sanctuary, we called each other almost daily to bounce around ideas. Early morning was the perfect time for Sam and me to touch base.

We were working through our horse rehoming to-do list, when I heard an almighty noise. It sounded like ripping metal.

'Holy heck,' I expleted down the phone.

Jim came barrelling down the hallway with a sleepy Leah and the five dogs in tow. 'Are you all right?' He looked at me wide-eyed.

We had no idea what had just happened. Jim dashed back out of the room and I picked up the phone receiver which I had dropped in shock.

I assured Sam that whatever it was it had passed and snuggled back down under the cosy duvet to talk horse again. I was in total denial that it really was time to get up and potentially something quite huge had just happened. The dogs had all burrowed under the duvet, which was a treat I allowed them when Jim wasn't looking, and I just didn't have the heart to kick them out so quickly.

A sodden Jim walked back into the bedroom, his face a mixture of panic and bewilderment.

'The roof's gone!'

I looked up at the celling, not able to process what he was saying. 'No it hasn't, it's right there.'

'Carolyn, the roof has blown off the house!'

'Sorry, Sam, I'll have to call you back.'

Okay, so we are pretty calm folk in hairy situations, but there was a very big question to answer . . . if the roof wasn't on our house, then where was it?

There was no time to get out of our pyjamas so we threw on our gumboots and coats and ran outside. As we looked up through the pelting rain it was clear from the exposed rafters that Jim's assessment was right. But our sense of urgency was for the animals and their safety.

First stop was the monkey garage, only ten metres downwind from the house. Phew, they were completely unaware and happily waiting for their breakfast. We ran beyond the garage and there, about 60 metres away from its place of origin, precariously balanced on a fence, half on the chicken coop and half in the horse paddock, was our roof.

Holy moley! I went to call the fire brigade for help.

It's a little embarrassing causing such a stir in the community, especially when there was already a stir about us, but as the daylight grew it was hard to miss the predicament we were in up on top of our little hill. I placed the receiver down and assured Jim that the fire brigade was on its way. Then I noticed the celling starting to sag. Jim set about punching holes in it to allow the water to pour through, then set about drilling holes in the floorboards for it to escape. As we worked our way around the house we assessed that only the laundry, Shaun's room and our bedroom still had enough roof to keep us dry. The rest of the house was a write-off. I could see flashing lights coming up the drive and behind the fire engine were two civilian cars. As the firemen emerged from their vehicles in full wet-weather gear, sauntering up behind them was a familiar face in a Swanndri and shorts. It was Skin, the owner of Jane the pig, and he was hauling the hugest tarp I have ever seen.

With all hands on deck it only took an hour or so to secure the massive tarp over the house. It was clear the house had sustained a lot of damage but there was no time to dwell on it so Jim and I set about feeding the animals and getting ready for court. Yes, today was the day that our scary neighbours were taking us to the Disputes Tribunal over our shared driveway. Oh what fun!

The angry neighbours had lined the shared driveway with pea metal that they had scored from a mate as a perky and we were led to believe that they had only had to reimburse their friend with some beer for the metal. They had done the work without consultation or agreement from either us or our nice neighbours, and then taken us to the tribunal because we refused to pay our 'share', which would have seen them receive a very tidy and not entirely kosher profit.

As we sat in the small room awaiting the decision there was an awkward silence. We were seated on one side of the table with our nice neighbours, and the angry neighbours were on the other, with the adjudicator at the head of the table like a parent figure.

The adjudicator had heard both sides of the story and explained to us all that we did not need to pay for the driveway and that the angry neighbours also needed to understand that we had full unrestricted use of the driveway and they could not control our visitors. He looked them in the eye and said, 'I think Mr McKenzie and Mrs Press have enough on their plates today without you wasting their and all of our time.'

As we came up the driveway a few hours later we were followed by an insurance assessor. He came prepared in gumboots and a heavy raincoat and as he walked around the house his disgruntled tutting was audible.

'There were no Zed nails securing the roof?' He looked perplexed.

We each held our breath. We seriously had no idea—we

had thought that the shiny new roof was the only thing our tired old house had going for it. Who would cut back on something like roof fastenings? We were horrified and terrified . . . what if the insurance company refused to pay? We'd be physically homeless and financially ruined.

'Well, you are going to need about $100,000 of repairs and it should take about three months. First things first, you need to book into a motel.'

Jim and I looked at each other with complete relief—they were going to help us.

'But we can't leave the animals,' Jim explained.

'What about a motor home parked on the driveway?' I pitched in.

And so that was that for the next three months; Jim and I and the kids (when they were with us every other week) camping on the driveway! It took me back to the old days when I was living in my bus. I was in heaven, though it became very apparent very quickly that I was the only one.

It was winter and in the cold and harsh weather the motor home developed a knack for sweating and growing mould on the inside. We were all sick, permanently cold, crooked and cramped. But we were grateful to be at home and to watch our house slowly but surely coming back to life. It was alarming how many things needed fixing. Who knew that the house had absolutely no insulation in it, but the insurance company was required by law to rebuild to current building code standards which meant we got insulation bats. In fact, our house looked somewhat further along than it had been before the incident.

And once again we learnt that with every bad situation there is a shiny silver lining. No one had been hurt, we now had a warm and cosy house, Rachel had the wet and ruined remains of the inside of our house to climb over and explore right on our front lawn, and the lovely Greek folk at the local fish and chip shop were so excited to tell us that our disaster had made it on to the international news for all their family in Greece to see.

Everyone was happy.

CHAPTER 25

Rachel

Whether she realised it at the time or not, Leah had a pretty extraordinary childhood for a young Kiwi girl.

On lazy sunny weekend mornings Jim and I would tether Rachel on a long lead outside Leah's bedroom window. It was a safe and sunny spot for Rachel to have her breakfast, looking over the wonderful and enchanting view of the valley. Being a monkey, Rachel loved to climb things: trees, people, cars—she didn't care. She would often climb up the side of the house and perch, with her stinky Tigger toy firmly gripped in her foot, on the window ledge and look in the window at Leah sleeping. As Leah woke and stretched she would open her window and Rachel would climb through and together they would play on Leah's bed. I knew we wouldn't be able to do this for long because as soon as the new enclosure was built, Rachel would be assigned a new routine. But for now those magically innocent sunny mornings were of mutual benefit to both young ladies.

Rachel was different from the other monkeys. Actually, they were all completely different in age, looks, size and especially in personality. But Laurie and Charlie seemed to need us, perhaps because what we offered was a release from and a huge improvement on their awful past life. Rachel seemed as though she would never accept her fate as a captive animal. Unlike her travelling companions she was strong and vibrant; essentially her spirit had not been broken in the way theirs had.

I still thought a lot about Rachel's sister Joanna. It was hard to stomach that a monkey with as much strength and determination as her sister would die in such a sad and unnecessary way. I found it even harder to think of what her life had been like leading up to her death. I couldn't help but feel that maybe dying was her way of escaping such a heinous existence; in her reality, at only three years of age she had been facing another 30 years of captivity and control. But now, in heaven, her spirit was safe from being crushed and tortured . . . was Joanna the one who had really made it to freedom? The more we pondered the more we felt complete shame for mankind. We would do everything in our power to put the wrongs right, but ultimately no matter how much love and freedom we gave, we knew it would never be enough.

About six months after the monkeys arrived the ground had dried out and Jim had made good progress on their enclosures. One day we had a group of young school kids visiting and Rachel was sitting on shoulders and rummaging through the children's hair looking for nits, in her usually intense and bossy fashion. We noticed that one of her thumbs was sticking out on a right angle; it had somehow become dislocated.

It's a big deal taking your monkey to the vet in New Zealand. It requires a paper trail and high-security manoeuvring. But once we were settled safely at the vet clinic and assessing the X-rays, we knew it was worth the effort. Rachel needed to have a pin put in her crippled digit. This was a pretty straight-forward operation and we didn't hesitate with our decision to go ahead. With years of surgical nurse training under my belt I found it hard not to be at the steering wheel of the anaesthetic machine, so I stood at the head of the table assessing Rachel as the surgery progressed nicely. Jim, Shaun and Leah sat patiently in the waiting room, ready to be called in to hold her good hand when she woke.

Rachel's heart rate and breathing had been consistent and steady throughout the surgery. She had good colour and there were no alarm bells or signs to prepare us for what happened next. As the isoflorane gas was turned off and the oxygen continued to flow we intently waited for a reflex, a cue that she was waking and that it was safe to remove the tube from her trachea and place her in recovery. But nothing, no eye reflex, no gag reflex, not any reflex, nothing. As the healthy pink colour in her gums started to fade and her breathing became shallow, we cranked into action. The team working on Rachel was great and didn't miss a beat. They asked me to leave which I respected, and I sat with Jim and the kids numbly and quietly. We were in shock, and at a complete loss.

The vet, who also looked pale and shocked, came to talk to us. Rachel had passed. Would we like to hold her body? As Jim, Leah, Shaun and I sat on the floor of the surgery, we rocked her lifeless body gently and then each of us in turn held her tight and said goodbye. It was strange as it was the only time we had been able to hug her, really hug her.

We took Rachel home and buried her at the top of our hill overlooking the valley. We don't understand why she died that day. But a little part of me wonders if, like her sister Joanna, it was Rachel's way to escape, her chance to be free from captivity. She was larger than the life she had been dealt.

She had never allowed her spirit to be broken and she would never accept being caged.

Honestly, even with the best intentions, I don't think we could have ever truly made Rachel feel free and happy. We hope with all our hearts that she is in a better, kinder world now.

CHAPTER 26

Piggy Sue, three Burmese and a Chihuahua

Soon after we had moved to our ramshackle hill, Jim's mum followed us.

I often joked that I didn't have a gnome in the bottom of my garden for good luck, I had a mother-in-law in my bottom paddock instead. Jim's mum was wonderful, and Leah and Shaun loved the independence of trotting down the hill whenever they pleased to visit her in the little self-contained cottage that she had had built.

Grandma Carly's favourite story to tell about any of the animals that have come and gone from the sanctuary is that of a very special and slightly famous pig called Piggy Sue. For Grandma Carly this story is not about all the hype and fuss created around Piggy Sue's liberation from a life in a sow crate at a large commercial piggery. It is about what happened next, when the cameras stopped rolling.

Piggy had been with us no more than a week, and her stiff and awkward body, shaped by horribly cramped conditions, was starting to get used to the freedom of walking. She was becoming more animated and was falling into the routine of frolicking gaily behind Jim on the quad bike as he made his breakfast delivery. During the day she would explore the gullies and siesta the afternoon away, usually third in the line-up of six spooning pigs. One morning Grandma Carly called us on the telephone.

'You have to come and see this,' she said. 'Piggy Sue's discovered rain.'

I could hear the emotion and delight in Grandma Carly's voice so we all threw on our gumboots and rushed down the hill to share in the moment.

And there was Piggy Sue, not huddled away out of the weather with the other pigs, but nose in the air, dancing and prancing with the biggest smile on her face. Piggy Sue had had a roller-coaster week of firsts. And that morning was the first time she had ever felt the rain on her back, and she loved it.

The very next week I was flown by the animal advocacy group SAFE (Save Animals From Exploitation) to speak about my experience of saving Piggy Sue. I was going to be in the company of others such as Mike King and Robyn Malcolm who were speaking out against factory-farmed pigs. This is a summary of what I had to say.

My heart broke when we entered the intensive pig farm. The screaming and stench of 10,000 captive pigs was more shocking than I could ever have anticipated. I was wearing a hidden camera and microphone. My husband Jim and I had agreed to go undercover for Sunday for two reasons: to save one pig and to help expose an entire industry based on greed and cruelty. When five-year-old Piggy Sue arrived home at our 13-acre sanctuary she could barely walk and was emotionally switched off. The sadness in her eyes had matured from years of torment. Now just two weeks later she frolics and plays, she is an intelligent, curious and vital being. Thank you SAFE for helping Piggy Sue to find freedom. I only hope that New Zealanders have seen through our eyes and will fight alongside us to achieve this much needed change in legislation.

We enjoyed watching Piggy Sue love every second of her freedom for three more years. Then sadly, one morning, at the age of eight, she just didn't wake up. But we find solace in the fact that she died in her very own little piece of paradise surrounded with love, not caged and lonely and surrounded in fear.

Vicki from the Wellington pound is a legend. She doesn't fit the stereotype of an animal control officer who is out to punish animals and their people. She strives harder than most to save lives and she is good at what she does. It's certainly not an easy job, certainly one that I don't envy. The sheer volume of animals dumped weekly at the pound is enough to send anyone to rock in a corner, devastated. And yet Vicki is somehow able to balance out the trauma of the ones that are destroyed by helping as many as she possibly can. Thanks to Vicki, her colleague Jane and now several of their associates, we talk almost daily, planning and stargazing, trying to find as many positive outcomes as we can for the animals left at the pound.

Right at the beginning of our relationship Vicki called me to ask if I knew of anyone who would be prepared to take on three Burmese cats.

'They come with an inheritance,' she added, just in case it made a difference.

The owner was not expected to live for much longer and the family were at their wits' end over what to do with her animals. Vicki had already found a safe and loving home for the lady's three Labradors, but the cats were proving more difficult.

'We'll take them, Vicki.' I didn't hesitate. We had plenty of room and a particular soft spot for oriental breeds. I followed up with a laugh. 'And no, it's not because of the inheritance!' And of course I meant it.

As I met with Vicki to collect the precious bundles she explained that one of the three was missing. Lucy, the youngest of the cats, had left home when her owner had been taken to hospital, and despite everyone's best efforts to find her she had not yet come home. Vicki then asked me for a favour. The family wanted to know more about us, so that they could tell the owner, who was now in a coma, that it was okay to pass, and that her much-loved pets were safe.

This is what we wrote.

Although we have never met we are about to have something very important in common, three very special cats.

I wanted to write to you, to tell you how much I admire you for being guardian to these beautiful animals. It is clear to me how much they have loved you, and been loved by you. It is distressing to think that you are leaving this world, but please feel comfort in the knowledge that your precious animal family is safe and loved. As I write, Hugo is investigating his new home with us, though he has spent most of his new adventure rolling on his back purring and attacking his scratch post with great passion. Sylvie has made friends with Leah, my 13-year-old step-daughter, and is already snuggled into bed with her. It is just Lucy that we need to settle but I am confident that she will love it here too.

We live on an animal sanctuary on 13 beautiful acres of rolling paddocks and native bush. It truly is an adventure-filled paradise for all animals. It is up a very long driveway so your family will be safely away from the road.

As well as having a people family to love, Hugo, Sylvie and Lucy will be living with some other special characters including five dogs, three elderly cats, a very bossy parrot, two ex-circus monkeys and various precious farm animals and horses, all of whom came to us to live out their lives in safety and with lots of love.

I want to promise to you that your friends are wanted and will be treasured. We will always speak of you, your memory will not be forgotten. We will tend to their needs and make sure there is always fun and plenty of sunshine for them.

We will never replace the home or the memories they shared with you, but we will give them a new home and new memories. We will love them and protect them.

Thank you for caring enough to keep them together. Please be assured that they will always have each other. If you are able to watch over them I am sure you will be smiling.

Vicki and the family tried for months to find Lucy, but she never materialised. We often think of her. Hugo, who shortly after his arrival was diagnosed with diabetes, passed away several years later. Sylvie, now nineteen years old, is sitting on my knee as I write, purring and content.

As I drove to meet a lady and her wee sick puppy I was rocked by what she had told me. She had bought the pup just a few days before from the same pet shop that Haggis had come from. They had moved premises and opened a flash new mega-store on the other side of town, but they still had the awful original building and that's where they kept the underage pups before putting them into the shiny new glass-fronted display cabinets of their shiny new store.

The lady who called me had been up all night sitting in the waiting room of a vet clinic, while nurses and vets worked on her new puppy as it seizured and drifted in and out of consciousness. The vets diagnosed that the tiny little Chihuahua puppy was underage and not robust enough to be away from her mum. They said that the fitting through the night had been triggered when the puppy's blood sugar had fallen so dangerously low that she had become hypoglycaemic. She survived the night but the little pup would need constant care and attention to ensure she was eating enough calories, little and often.

As I pulled up to the parking lot she was ready and waiting with the puppy swaddled in a pretty pink and white fleecy blanket.

'Hi, Joan! Aww, gosh she is absolutely tiny.' I couldn't help but smile at the miniature bundle in front of me. She was so little and delicate, and her soft brown eyes were struggling to stay open as she nestled safely in Joan's arms.

'Thank you for coming.' Joan was already emotional. 'I just didn't know what else to do.'

Joan is a businesswoman, very driven, intelligent and busy, and I had helped her once before by taking in a stray cat from her neighbourhood, then desexing and rehoming it. She explained that when she had visited the pet store for cat food just days ago she had been completely taken by the little puppy sitting alone in the cabinet. The staff had been quick to tell her that it didn't matter that she worked full-time, a lovely home like hers was just what the puppy needed, and the sale was made.

'Can you please take her? I just don't think I can do this.' Joan was a mess; this lovely woman was facing a huge and unfair dilemma. She hadn't been shopping for a puppy that day, but those little soft brown eyes had drawn her in. The staff at the store had told Joan that the puppy was eight weeks old. I frowned, and felt vexed. There is no law about the minimum age that puppies can be sold from a pet store, however there is a code of welfare recommendation that states that selling a puppy at eight weeks is acceptable. But this sort of thing makes me so angry; sure, eight weeks may be okay for a Labrador pup at a pinch, but this tiny little girl was only just a few hundred grams and clearly not robust or advanced enough to cope away from her mum, and especially not her litter mates.

As Joan passed the puppy over, she explained that she was within her rights to ask for a refund but that she just couldn't stomach returning the dog to the store. She had also realised that she wasn't equipped to care for the pup and all its needs and demands. While her impulse purchase had seemed like a nice idea at the time, she had been romanced into the idea that the pup and her cat would be smiling and waiting for her when she got home from work each night, and truly hadn't realised the implications of buying the puppy.

Jim's reaction to our new charge was quite entertaining. He was totally entranced by the fragile little pup. It was the weekend and instead of catching up on farm chores, he sat on the couch with the tiny Chihuahua snuggled up inside his jumper. As I wandered past Jim throughout the day, I'd catch him grinning at her little face and her little paws and babbling baby talk as he gently cradled her. On one walkby I caught him holding her up in the air with both hands singing the *Lion King* theme tune. And then he proudly announced that he was calling her Lily. I only just managed to drag her away from him to feed her in between sleeps. And when

Jim headed off to work on Monday it was with a very long face.

As Lily grew stronger and more robust we realised she had small but unimportant faults, like two rows of incisor teeth, which were an indication of the sort of breeding facility she had possibly come from.

After Joan had passed Lily over that day I had set about getting more information on the pet store, and as luck would have it I actually knew someone who worked there, and she was prepared to pass on information. Stacey and I had crossed paths at a workplace several years earlier. We didn't know each other well, but she, too, was concerned about the age of the puppies for sale and decided that she couldn't stomach turning a blind eye and was ready to speak out.

I called the SPCA inspectors straight away and relayed all of the information I had been given. Stacey had told me there was a constant flow of puppies coming into the store. She said that as well as the old store, they also had a small room out the back where they held the pups in quarantine for a few weeks until they were old enough to put in the display cabinets. She said it was not uncommon for the pups to fade and die, and they would just replace them with new ones. I was so relieved when the inspectors told me that there was enough information to warrant a visit to the store. I waited anxiously for their call.

'Well, you're right, there are a lot of puppies,' said the inspector. He then went on to explain that aside from asking them to address some airflow issues there was not much he could do. The sick pups out the back were getting veterinary care and the underage ones, while being too young morally, were of legal age. New Zealand's *Animal Welfare Act* did not protect them from being sold. It was a frustrating situation and both the SPCA and I agreed it was one we should keep a very close eye on.

Back home Lily and Jim were a firm team. As I watched Jim diligently teach Lily the art of riding on the front of the quad bike as he went about feeding all the farm animals, I smiled and accepted the fact that we had a new permanent member of the family.

CHAPTER 27

Good Morning

I couldn't quite believe it when one of the writers for the *Good Morning* TV chat show asked if I would like a regular slot presenting an animal corner.

I didn't know whether to laugh or cry. I could best describe what I was feeling as pretty much a mixture of horror and excitement with a healthy dollop of doubt thrown in. With some more convincing, I gingerly agreed and set about writing scripts for my up-and-coming slots.

I wasn't long at all before I absolutely loved this job. Every other Wednesday I would be present and correct with animals in tow for the live filming of my six- to eight-minute segment. I loved to mix things up and offer the viewers a visual variety of animals and topics. From chocolate toxicity to keeping your dogs cool when travelling in cars, an array of animal training tips to alpaca awareness, the slots were varied. But mostly I really loved the interactive segments, things like making home-made concoctions for bad breath, and enrichment toys. But when I put my serious hat on, it was the opportunity to educate that was so completely invaluable, allowing me to teach New Zealanders sensible tips to keep them and their pets safe.

My first appearance was pretty awful. My mouth was so dry from stage fright that speaking was hard, and with a camera pointed at my face, there just seemed to be no escaping the terror. But they invited me back and I started to relax and grow in confidence. The trick I learnt was to just ignore the camera and chat to the presenter the way I would chat to anyone picking my brain about an animal. Animals were what I knew about so there was no memorising tricky facts and figures; it all came down to talking from experience about my passion.

I'd have to rise at 4 a.m. to feed and settle the animals for the day and then package up whichever animal was to be my model for the day and off we'd head to the studio. It was live television, so I'd be plonked into the hair and make-up chair and they would work their wonders . . . then off to the green room and ready for action.

The animals I took with me were carefully chosen. I didn't want them to stress so I cast them as I would have done for a movie. Pixie and Punga came to demonstrate hoof care and laminitis. Tracey and Steve next door loaned me their alpaca and Tracey for an alpaca care segment. And Haggis, Ned and Lily, Norm and Tucker took turns, helping me cover every dog topic I could come up with.

Norm had come to our family at just sixteen weeks old, a year or so after Murphy had died. We had chosen him from an ethical breeder who only allowed Norm's mum to have the one litter before desexing her. Although we are surrounded by rescues and would never usually go out and buy a dog, Jim and I felt one exception could be justified because we so absolutely love pure-bred bull mastiffs, their nature and their classic mastiffy traits. We also feel it's important that ethical breeding of pure breeds is continued and encouraged—it's the irresponsible backyard breeders that get our blood boiling, as you will come to learn loud and clear.

Norm was the dog version of Drum; big, slow and squishy, and everyone who met the impressive beast that was Norm instantly fell in love with his calm and gentle manner. I learned quickly that he was a show stealer. As I diligently explained important topics to the New Zealand viewers, the camera would roam away from me and whatever I was doing and rest on Norm, usually so relaxed that he would be upside down, legs in the air and either snoring or farting. He was a hit and the crew always looked disappointed if I didn't bring Norm along for at least a visit.

We joked that Tucker was Norm's puppy. We had found him at a farm, where Tucker's mum had fallen pregnant to the wrong dog and as a result his litter was not wanted. We called this baby tri-coloured heading dog crossed with a huntaway Tucker because he threw up his tucker as we drove him home over the Rimutakas. To Norm, he was the best apprentice a dog could ever have, and in our view the benefits worked both ways. With Ned and Haggis more invested in me and what I was up to, the two youngsters merged their alliances and became as one. Eight years later they still jam in one dog bed together.

Tucker's role on *Good Morning* was an important one. He was to be trained and raised under the watchful eyes of New Zealand. It was my dream come true to be able to explain important values and techniques in such an interactive way. I was assigned a wonderful presenter, who would play the role of a clueless dog owner who needed to be taught the ropes and he was perfect . . . mostly because he was clueless on the subject of dogs! He'd ask typical new-owner questions which I would answer, expelling myths or by demonstrating with Tucker to give a wonderfully visual explanation.

My other favourite *Good Morning* star was Agnes the cat. I would often get praised for how well behaved Agnes was; before, during and after filming Agnes would just sit, happily relaxed, with her tongue hanging out in an adorable way, and dribble. The crew would tell me that they had never seen a cat trained so well. She was quite the hit and I was quite the legend . . . that is until I fessed up that my loved and treasured Agnes had come into my care at the sanctuary with muscular dystrophy. She was, and is, disabled, and thoroughly enjoyed the outing, but was not able to walk well or fast. So she would just opt to sit and enjoy the heat of the studio lights and all the wonderful attention, deliriously happy.

After my third year of *Good Morning*, the show relocated to Auckland so I ultimately lost that job. But I will always be grateful to the researcher who found me and gave me the opportunity to teach and be heard.

CHAPTER 28

Henry the heron

Isn't it funny how there is no rhyme or reason to falling in love? Well, the same applies to rescuers and the animals they care for.

Dealing with hundreds of animals in need every year, you invest your love and time into all of them. You work hard to find each and every one a positive outcome. It's not cool to have favourites or even to be species-ist, because they all rely on you to help them survive and find a safe future. But every once in a while you meet an animal that digs just a little deeper into your heart. For me, one of my great loves was a wonky little bird named Henry the heron.

We had been rehabilitating native wildlife for several years. In fact, I first got Department of Conservation approval when I was back on my bus. Becoming an approved rehabber had essentially involved proving to the department that I was serious and that I was capable. Serious enough to understand the importance of native wildlife and serious enough to understand the importance of not imprinting the wildlife in my charge—meaning that wherever possible they were to remain wild and would be released when fit, not conditioned or kept as pets. I also had to show that I was capable enough to learn and grow my skills. Over the years we have rehabbed a huge variety of native wildlife, from ruru to kakas and everything in between. Despite the very strong opinion of one very publicly outspoken Mr Gareth Morgan, most injuries are not from 'pesky cats' but from weather blasts leading to exhaustion, hitting power lines which injure their wings, or flying into windows, fracturing their shoulder blades and causing head injuries. Or they're just from simple viruses and infection.

Working with nature is such a rewarding thing to do. The hard yards with rehabilitating domestic or farm animals is that you have to rehome them, to entrust the rest of their lives to other people, which, no matter how thorough you are, can be scary. Even after myriad checks and procedures, how do you truly know that the new adoptive parents really do have the capability and follow-through to protect that animal and keep it happy and out of harm's way?

Although animals in captivity and animals in the wild are both very vulnerable, in captivity they are essentially always controlled by and reliant on humans. The margin for error is huge; I can't forget all the mistakes I have been personally accountable for on my own journey of animal ownership— and I'd like to think I was one of the good ones! Although the wild is ultimately affected by humans too, releasing a living being into an environment with no cages and no direct human contact, interference or manipulation somehow seems to sit easier; just fly, be free and cross your fingers that they stay well away from danger.

Henry, however, was not one of the lucky ones. He had

been born with a deformity that meant cages and humans were his only hope of survival. Henry's condition was something called 'scissor beak', which is the misalignment of the top and bottom parts of his beak. Instead of closing flush, his beak permanently stayed splayed. He could open and shut his beak but being a heron with a long thin elegant bill, the top portion curved out to the left and the bottom out to the right and never the twain did meet. This meant Henry had to be hand-fed every day for the rest of his life.

We were honoured to be chosen as Henry's caregivers. He had lived with a local bird rehabilitating legend for nine years, but when this bird man was tragically diagnosed with cancer we had been chosen by his wife to continue caring for their much-loved Henry.

We decided that the best place to house him was in the monkey's old circus enclosure, which we had permanently erected around a turtle pond. It was in constant use as a flight run for recovering kereru and other injured wildlife.

Henry was in heaven. His long stilt-like legs would stalk around the pond as he looked for bugs and creatures. He'd peck with full gusto at the little tasty-looking morsels, but his wonky beak meant that even the most accurately timed swipe would come up empty. Jim and I often grimaced at our dedication to these creatures. We both had been staunch vegans for several years now and yet every morning while preparing the feeds we would defrost one-day-old chicks (sent to us by the zoo) for the ruru, and once a week divvy out cannon bones for the dogs—there was no avoiding it. And with the arrival of Henry came the age of the ox-heart strips, carefully sliced into thin worm-like slithers and dangled in front of Henry so he could hook them in his beak, swing them back like a pendulum into his mouth and swallow them whole.

The reason I loved Henry so was because his grumpy façade was just that, a façade. He was a proud bird and worked the pond with the confidence of a movie star. Every morning he'd honk at me in a bossy fashion then stand poised and awaiting service. But what I really admired about Henry was his ability to accept and make friends. The first was Bubble 07, a rescued terrapin with whom he shared the pond, and most recently Charlie, the just as grumpy on the outside and squishy in the middle old monkey. The three spent hours upon hours together in the tranquillity of the flight run. As the days heated up Charlie would lie stretched out sunning himself, with his arthritic old legs spread for optimum exposure. Bubble 07 would park up next to Charlie with a right-side-up turtle version of the pose alongside the water's edge. And Henry waded with the determination of a dedicated fisherman in the water. Their friendship warmed our souls like nothing else.

Each of these unusual animals had lost their families somewhere along the way, but together they seemed content. There was no hugging or grooming each other, just a content mutual acceptance and companionship that brought a little bit of magic to their lives.

CHAPTER 29

A different way of thinking

We couldn't believe our ears when we were told that there was a petition circulating throughout the community listing all the reasons we should be closed down.

We knew the ringleaders, our scary neighbours, had been stirring things up, but this was seriously taking things too far. They had even got one neighbour in such a spin that she believed we were getting a circus elephant and had already called her insurance provider to enquire about stampede insurance!

Back then, Steve and Tracey were really the only ones who truly knew us. We had one other set of direct neighbours but they moved out soon after the dispute. Steve and Tracey didn't share the contentious driveway with us, but they did share several hundred metres of boundary and our children played together as they grew up. We had also rehomed a number of farm animals to them over the years, and respected and appreciated the care they gave them. Steve and Tracey would sit on the sidelines and, intrigued, watch the drama that we managed to cause in the community unfold without us doing anything except keep to ourselves. So as the news of the latest hot gossip rolled in we would be invited for a cup of tea and a laugh. It is easy to fob it all off and joke about it on the outside, but if we were to be honest, Jim and I were completely crushed by the attitude of the neighbours. We were vegan and we had monkeys; I think we sounded pretty cool. But in a community that farmed animals clearly we weren't.

The petition was quite the read. The two points that really stood out were the claims that our new monkey enclosures were an eyesore and we should not have been allowed to build them, and that there was a real risk that monkey faeces would contaminate the river and render valuable farm stock sick. Pretty ironic, we thought, when farming has been implicated as the main polluter of New Zealand waterways for years. The real kicker was that the river closest to us was over 600 metres away from the enclosures, and even the monkeys, as clever as they were, couldn't throw that far.

But 35 locals had decided that we were a concern and signed the petition to get the council to take action against us. We ended up at a council hearing where we had to defend the sanctuary, our animals and ourselves. Luckily, the council saw sense, and made it official by awarding us a resource consent to carry on doing what we were doing. I guess that didn't make us any more popular with some of our neighbours and aside from the ever supportive Steve and Tracey and their Brady Bunch of kids, we felt very much alone.

Well, we thought we were alone, but that's when things started to change some more.

I had decided that sponsorship should be a top priority for HUHA, to try to bring in some much-needed money on a regular and reliable basis. We already had a few sponsors who donated $5 a week or up to $40 a month for a particular animal they had chosen, and in return we would send them thank-you letters, an invitation to visit the animal and a tax receipt so they could claim for a charitable donation. Sponsorship, even today, is our lifeblood; it's what helps us pay the bills and keep the animals cared for.

And way back in the beginning it is also what brought us Vari and Taylor. Vari and Taylor are mother and daughter, and for months they had been sponsoring Pixie the pony. They were really hands-on and the two of them would visit every few weeks to brush Pixie and take her for walks. They loved it, Pixie loved it and we loved it. Their support helped on every level.

Soon after Vari and Taylor came Shaz and Val who also started to sponsor and visit Yogi the kune kune, and then there was Issi and Anne, two sisters from the Kapiti Coast who signed up to volunteer picking up horse poo and pulling ragwort. Although the latter four didn't visit regularly, when they did we really valued their contribution. That's what I love about HUHA; people can start with simple curiosity and dip their toe in the water. There is no pressure, just a grateful and welcoming attitude for any sort of help or attention given to the animals. And as the HUHA magic starts to take hold it is not uncommon for casual visits to turn into more, and soon people find themselves addicted.

But there was something different about all of these ladies. They seemed to be somehow more in tune with our vision and were drawn to our ideas and values, and most of all there was no denying that they were drawn to the animals. Little did we know at the time, but over the next few years these special ladies, together with Sam and a few more HUHArians we were yet to meet, were to be our segue into the next and most exciting phase of HUHA. It was my dream to grow and change our way of thinking to 'we' not 'me', to be sustainable and a true force to be reckoned with. My instincts told me that letting go, sharing and welcoming newcomers was the key.

They would be our future.

CHAPTER 30

Community Max

Still handling the day-to-day running of the shelter on our own, Jim and I were a tight team.

Not everyone got to see the soft side of him though. At first glance he was a bit like Henry the heron, but without the movie-star strutting. With Jim you had to earn his respect. Lately, we had been struggling. We were out of money and still as overwhelmed as ever. I was locum nursing and bringing in a few hundred dollars every week to supplement Jim's wages, but I seemed to have more and more work at home and less time for the paying job. In turn Jim was having to take on more and more overtime to make up for my shortfall. But no matter how many hours Jim put in we still seemed to be going backwards and he was becoming understandably depressed and exhausted.

Despite our best efforts to get out into the community and educate folk, we were still being used as a dump-and-run station. Although some donations trickled through and our sponsorship programme was starting to take shape, we had to cope with most of the costs on our own. And the pressure of keeping both our family and the sanctuary afloat was slowly tipping Jim over the edge. My mum and Vari had started to take turns dropping off care packages to keep us fed.

Then one phone call changed everything.

The caller was asking if we would be interested in becoming involved in a government initiative called Community Max. Essentially we would have a group of young unemployed people working for us full-time for six months. We would have to apply for a grant from Work and Income New Zealand (WINZ) which would cover their wages as well as the wages of one supervisor for every four youths. All applicants would be put forward by WINZ and we would hire the workers via the usual interview process. The young people would be aged between 16 and 24 years, and have a history of not successfully finding work.

As I listened to what the caller had to say, I pondered the possibilities, then I called Jim and ran the idea past him. 'What do you think? Should we do it?' I tend to have a cup-half-full approach when pitching an idea to Jim, who is less trusting of change.

Jim had just built the monkey enclosures all on his own, every steel pole and every link of chain mesh hauled up a steep hill and pieced together using nothing but his own strength and determination. Jim's work ethic is tireless, and he is also a bit of a perfectionist. We had held several working bees in the past, but usually attracted the peace and love, nuts and berries type of folk, who liked to cuddle animals but were not quite the handy types we so desperately needed. So at the end of each working bee, as we waved goodbye to the visitors, I'd see Jim dash back into the paddocks to rework or repair their efforts. He was in a constant state of frustration and held the very strong opinion that it was better if he just did everything properly himself.

'We can have twelve of them,' I marvelled. 'And I will be paid as one of the three supervisors!'

It was a dream to think that for six months I would be able to work full-time rescuing and rehabilitating with no interruptions, and to bring in my share of the money we needed to survive. But Jim worried about the calibre of the employees, worried that the animals would be safe and worried that I would be safe.

'You know what, Jim?' I put my practical hat on. 'We work so hard because of the folk in the community who are in a constant state of ignorance when it comes to animals and their care . . . this is our chance to teach them. Every kid we teach will go home and teach their family and friends.'

I paused for effect and to let my sage words sink in, then closed the deal with a take-no-prisoners, 'Let's do it.'

Who knew what we were getting ourselves into . . . we certainly didn't. And although it was quite an eye-opening and rocky journey, it was probably one of the most rewarding phases of our lives and our work. Taking on the scheme was a bit like a being in a reality TV show crossed with a soap opera. A huge dose of teenage-style drugs, sex and scandal were all heading our way, but we had big gumboots and had no problem stomping on anything that looked like trouble. Better still, we soon had them stomping out trouble too, because we gave them many more important productive things to think about and do. By involving these young people in saving animals' lives, they were ultimately saving their own.

The WINZ case officers had asked me to write up job descriptions and then set me up in an interview room. First step was to hire the supervisors who could help me wrangle the young ones. I needed one admin supervisor, one building supervisor and I would supervise the animal care as well as oversee the whole operation. The second step was to hire the workers. I had shown the WINZ people the three job category descriptions, each requiring a different set of skills: admin, building and animal care. The plan was to hire four people for each job area.

The interviews were interesting, and each applicant came with a different set of dramas.

'I can't drive because I've just come out of prison.'

'I can't touch animals because I'm allergic, but I really like them.'

'I can't work in mud because I only wear high heels.'

'Are your animals dirty?'

'Do youse have any pitbulls?'

It became very apparent very quickly that these kids did not know how to put their best foot forward in an interview, with most of them having a 'me me me' line of thinking. I didn't know who they had been using as role models, but it was very clear why they didn't yet have a job. But we managed to pick our twelve, a hugely diverse bunch of characters, most of whom came coupled with drug, alcohol and driving convictions. There was also one prison parolee and one convicted computer hacker who had been too young at the time to be charged.

I was in heaven. I had wonky kids to rehabilitate with the wonky animals, and I could see the good in them all.

I had asked a newbie to the neighbourhood to come on board as the admin supervisor. She was a godsend and helped to make sense of the truckload of paperwork that came with having so many employees. She also cracked the admin team into shape and got them started on improving our IT system, initiatives and sponsorship programme.

I really had no idea what they were talking about when I walked into the makeshift office in our spare room and the team asked for my permission to set up a HUHA Facebook page.

'I guess so . . . Can you explain to me what it is again?'

This social networking thing was a completely foreign concept to me.

Their first attempt to set up HUHA on Facebook was unsuccessful. They had put us in the wrong category or something, so when they told me that they needed to start again and we needed a new name I just stared blankly at them.

'We can't have a new name—HUHA is our name.'

The debate went back and forth for a while and eventually we compromised. To this day we are known on Facebook not as HUHA but HUHANZ.

I decided that now we were social-media savvy I would get the team to organise an event to raise our profile. I wanted to it to be something for the wider community, to give them a chance to see who we were and what we were about. I also wanted to give the kids a project to focus on and learn from—maybe I enjoy watching *The Vicar of Dibley* too much and have a sad longing for that sort of community spirit in Kaitoke. Whatever the reason I was completely romanced with the idea of organising a giant pumpkin-growing competition. My mother wrote children's books and one of her stories was about a country fair with a pumpkin harvest. I loved this story and having a pumpkin-growing competition had long been a dream of mine.

I got on the phone and did a ring around, ordering in 300 giant pumpkin seeds . . . oh, it was just too exciting! It was November and there was plenty of time to get those seeds dispersed throughout the community and growing into giant pumpkins.

The admin team busied themselves putting together a plan of attack. They needed to develop a way to engage the community and rally a healthy competitive spirit. With our website and Facebook page they were able to promote to the masses and they also took posters and envelopes containing three seeds each to sell for $2 at the local supermarket checkouts in Upper Hutt. All the packets of pumpkin seeds sold, and the buzz of the up-and-coming competition began to gather momentum. The workers had also dropped packets of seeds off to the primary schools, who set about planting them with great delight.

In between scrub cutting and constructing fences at the sanctuary, the building team had the task of making sign-posts and display stands; they even made some carnival-type games that they could set up on the day of the competition.

As well as doing their routine animal care chores, the animal team were kept busy growing pumpkins—gigantic pumpkins—which was just so rewarding and exciting.

As summer emerged orphaned baby animals started to find their way into our care. Sadly, baby animal season is our busiest time of year, and soon the team was rushed off their feet, bordering on overloaded. A baby goat whose mother had been shot by a hunter followed the building team around when it wasn't being bottle fed by its new and attentive caregivers. Litters of kittens, puppies and even bunnies were set up in collapsible crates in the admin room and baby birds were on an hourly feeding roster.

The team doted on the newcomers with the precision of skilled professionals. The rest of the animal crew, including the monkeys, the remaining and now elderly motley crew, Pixie's wee family and Henry and his harem of kereru and turtles, was loving the attention. And Jim was quietly impressed . . . even with the building work.

One of the extra special babies to arrive that summer was a little fussy yellow pom-pom of a duckling we called Cecil. He came to us on his own, which is never a good thing for ducklings as by themselves they often get depressed and fade away. So some quick thinking out of the square saw him snuggled up in the admin room with his new brothers and sisters: four warm, soft and fluffy baby bunnies. He happily cuddled into them and with their heartbeats close he was content and a sure survivor.

When the building boys came in for lunch and puzzled at the strange combination of Muscovy duckling and baby bunnies, I smiled and suggested they look around. There on the lawn just outside the window the kid goat was sunbathing with the dogs. In the next paddock Weemu the Emu was hanging with her best friend Bernie the Sheep. Piggy Sue was leaned up against Mabel the cow and Henry, of course, was having a lovely day wading among the turtles in his pond. I told the kids to cast a wider eye and to study the farm land that surrounded us.

'What do you see?' I asked.

'Cows?' one replied

I pointed at another paddock. 'And there?'

'Sheep?'

'Exactly,' I said. 'People have separated them for farming purposes and now that is our perceived normal, but given the chance all animals are social creatures . . . it's we humans who keep them in their categories and boxes.'

I watched the kids as they went back to work, each of them stopping for a moment to pat or tickle an animal on the way. They were surrounded by the magic of animals and as I watched them start to think and soften, I knew it was having an effect. These kids were starting to realise that there was more to the world than just their little bubble. They were starting to consider and think about others.

The end of March rolled around, and the day of the competition was horribly cold. But we had organised so much fun and we would not let a bit of bad weather rain on our parade. The building team set up trestle tables and signs, as well as the stands for the giant pumpkins to be displayed on and judged. We had been given permission to use the local Kaitoke Country Gardens, which came complete with a mock manor-style wedding venue and café; it was a very flash faux brick building with elegant arched windows and extensive gardens.

We were so excited when the locals started wheeling in their giant specimens. Some of the team manned the large scales that we had borrowed for the day and there would be loud whoop-whoops as each pumpkin was weighed and then placed in the judging line-up.

For those who had not grown a pumpkin, we had face painting, an animal corner containing Cecil the duckling and his fluffy bunny siblings, a pumpkin pie competition and a pumpkin-carving competition. We had spent months collecting prizes donated by local businesses. One local company had made very fancy ribbons for the prize winners. The place looked amazing—my *Vicar of Dibley* dream made real!

The community came in droves: mums and dads with their kids, grandmas and granddads and even teachers bringing their pupils. I looked at my team. They had achieved something truly special and memorable and I knew they would never forget what they had done.

The fun didn't stop when we waved the last of the visitors goodbye. Now it was time to take all of the donated pumpkins—and boy, were there a lot of pumpkins—back to the sanctuary for the animals to enjoy. And none more so than Piggy Sue who wore an orange smile for days to come.

Outside in the building department, I was sure that the supervisor was higher than the employees—and I don't mean in rank. He spent a lot of time grinning, was always ping-ponging from exceptionally cruisy and laid back to uptight and intolerant, and seemed to have permanently bloodshot watery eyes. The kids, though, were on fire, and we set about picking some projects for them to get into. There were shelters to build, old manuka and gorse to clear and more fences to build. Among their haphazard styles and talents they were really getting into it and taking pride in their work. The animals were in on everything, up on everyone's business and making it all about them. This kept them and their needs forefront of everyone's minds, which I believe is what made it work. And the supervisor? Well, in the end we accepted his resignation.

We did, however, have regular mishaps as some aspects of the Community Maxers' personal lives came with them to work. One poor chap was often found in the bush with a bottle of something strong. After the third time he was asked to leave and we ensured that he received the ongoing help he needed. There were a couple of romances that took place in the bush also, so we separated the hormoned-up offenders and kept them busy, advising them to wait until they got home!

I was excited to give the animal team the opportunity to go on a road trip to rescue some battery hens. On this occasion the kids got a rare glimpse inside a battery barn because the owner was too lazy to catch the hens we had ordered. The chicken man had looked the kids up and down and seemed to judge them as his kind of people. He probably assumed that the state of the chooks would mean nothing to them and that like him they were the sort of human beings who put money and food before welfare. As a result he didn't hide the reality of what lay behind the barn doors. So, as each 'spent and useless' sixteen-month-old chicken was dragged upside down by its leg from its overcrowded prison cell, pecked bald and bullied for its entire existence, the sombre kids stood by with a cat box to transport it back to the ute.

On the way home I asked the kids how they felt.

'Jeeze, I've never seen anything like that. Do we seriously eat that shit? It stank. How could he let them live like that?' said Jack, who was fresh out of prison.

I wondered if he saw the connection between the experience he had just lived through and what these chooks had lived through.

I was delighted when the workers asked me if they could produce a YouTube video about their experience so they could tell people where their eggs came from, and I said that I thought it was a lovely idea. So they set about making the video with the hope that it would help with factory-farming awareness. They were serious and on a mission, which is not an unexpected response when people see ex-battery hens for the first time. Aside from saving their lives, this is the very reason we liberate the chooks. Spreading the word within the community once the chooks have been visited by shocked family and neighbours is invaluable.

CHAPTER 31

Laurie gets his Jungle

We were still dealing with the end of kitten season.

There had been a constant flow of kittens from people who wanted their kids to see a litter, or who had forgotten to desex their cat, or orphans whose mums had died or disappeared. They all needed to be bottle fed and eventually rehomed, and the team very quickly became masters at it. Once weaned, desexed and at ten weeks old we would advertise the kittens on Facebook. After checking all the new homes thoroughly, we would then wave a bittersweet goodbye.

One week towards the end of the season a wild kitten was dropped off. I asked the admin team if they would like to set up a dog crate by their desks so that the kitten could get used to people and movement. This is a technique called flooding, where you flood the animal with stimuli to help them get used to a busy environment and get over their fears. But as one of the girls leaned into the crate to stroke the little wild kitten, I decided on a change of plan.

The little tabby girl was only about five or six weeks old. She was quite sweet, but being born behind a supermarket had already given her street smarts and human interaction was not something she craved. As she hissed and spat at the team's efforts I couldn't help but admire how robust and confident she seemed, almost older and wiser than her years . . . well, her weeks.

'Let's try her with Laurie,' I announced. I thought it was a great idea for both monkey and kitten.

'Are you serious?' came a mixed chorus of surprise and excitement from around the room.

'Yip, I think she is just what Laurie needs—and I think he might just be the best thing to happen to her too.'

Just months before, we had finally managed to remove the collar and chain that was such a harsh reminder of Laurie's previous life. It was wonderful to get rid of them and it certainly made us feel better, but the odd thing was that in a very dysfunctional way it didn't seem to make Laurie feel better . . . well, not in the beginning anyway.

As part of his rite of passage in the circus, Laurie had had his canine teeth chopped or filed down. They were left blunt and the nerves exposed. He had clearly lived that way for years, maybe even more than a decade, but recently bilateral abscesses had developed under his chin and we needed to get him to the vets urgently to have all four canines removed. So while little Laurie was sleeping peacefully under anaesthetic we took the opportunity to remove his collar and chain.

When Laurie awoke, we expected him to feel confused and probably slightly violated that his teeth were gone, though we hoped that ultimately the relief from pain would make it worthwhile for him. What we hadn't expected was how completely shattered he was not to have his chain. He was a mess. He would sit away from us and scream, rocking back and forth and looking confused. He wanted to trust us but couldn't.

Laurie had grown so much confidence in his time with us, and part of that was because he felt like he had some control. If he wanted to interact he would pass us, and in particular his favourite person, Jim, his chain. And if he didn't want to spend time with us he would guard his chain with crossed arms and chatter nervously, cueing us to respect his privacy. But to Laurie, no chain meant no routine, no system, no control. He was a wreck. And to make matters worse, he blamed Jim. Before they'd had a bromance going on, but now he wouldn't let Jim near him. He clearly felt deeply betrayed.

So Laurie had been pretty inconsolable for months. He was now living full-time in his new enclosure. He had trees and forts and ropes and swings, but as far as social contact went, we were just the people who delivered the food and if we tried to engage any more than that he would slip into a panicked rage, frantically crossing his arms across his bare chest where the chain, his tool of communication, had once rested. Jim and I had learnt time and time again that in any situation involving an animal, patience is key. Laurie was safe, he was loved, he was more enriched than he had probably ever been in his sad and lonely life. He had us whenever he needed us, and although he was confused we knew that time would heal and eventually he would let us enrich his life more with our interactive company. But in the meantime I wondered if this little kitten could become someone special in Laurie's life.

So all fifteen of us excitedly waited for Jim to come home from work early so he and I could oversee the introduction together.

We knew that Laurie was gentle with other animals as he already lived with two giant Flemish bunnies that had been handed over to us one day. Jelly and Bean divided their time between Laurie and Charlie, happily hopping around their enclosures and mowing the lawns with a peaceful contentment and ease. They seemed none the wiser that it was not normal for bunnies to live with monkeys, and just appeared very happy to have the biggest bunny runs they had ever seen.

As Jim sat down and Laurie sat close by, I perched next to them with little Miss Hissy Spitty on my knee. Laurie saw her straight away and started to chatter and rock, holding his arms firmly crossed against his chest. He was nervous, but he was also interested. The bossy little kitten then jumped off my knee. She had zero interest in people and couldn't get herself away from me fast enough. Laurie inched closer to her, still chattering and swaying dysfunctionally, the way he always did when he felt out of his depth and out of control. Then it happened.

The kitten walked over to Laurie bold as brass and head-butted him gently in the leg. Laurie snapped out of his rocking immediately as if he had been slapped in the face by a friend telling him to calm down. He refocused on the little kitten, but this time instead of guarding his non-existent chain, he reached out and touched the kitten's back gingerly with one pointed finger, ET-style. 'Awww,' he said as the kitten continued to nudge him and rub up against him. 'Awww.' The kitten started to purr and Jim and I and the workers, looking on quietly from outside the enclosure, just smiled.

It took us about half an hour to settle on the name Jungle for the kitten.

'I know Laurie will never have a normal life,' I explained to the kids, 'but I like the idea of him having a jungle.'

Jungle and Laurie are a tight twosome: they eat together, sleep together, play and hunt together. They groom and sunbathe together. And the more their relationship grew in its early stages, the more they both relaxed around us. As Jungle matured she was allowed in and out of the enclosure. We have never caged her in, and her place of choice is with her best friend Laurie. Our little social experiment had worked; Laurie has his Jungle, but most importantly he has learned how to communicate and express himself without his chain.

CHAPTER 32

An emu, a pig, a turkey and Colonel Stinky

'Come on, team, we are on a mission,' I called out, as they all walked in the door early one morning.

A petting zoo had closed its doors and some of the older breeding stock needed saving. It was the usual story; all the purpose-bred babies, and the pretty and fancy animals, had been sold and the owners did not have the heart to kill the old breeding stock that had been keeping them in good supply of cute babes but were now deemed worthless.

Knowing that no animals are worthless to HUHA, they had asked us to come and collect the last of them. I never said no—we valued the animals' lives and would never begrudge a chance to save them—but as we had time and time again, we were starting to feel very used. I explained the situation to the kids as we drove there. Once we had these animals in our care, we would have the vet out and it was likely that we would easily spend a thousand dollars to desex and treat any medical problems that had gone unnoticed to date. Then these animals, the old and the ugly that the petting zoo themselves had deemed not fit for display, would stay in our care for some time while we looked for new homes. If no home was found then they were ours. So one quick phone call from this business to off-load and ease their guilt, in reality, was about to cost us several years of time, money and commitment. We didn't mind doing it for the sake of the animals; we just quietly wished that folk appreciated what their actions and constant breeding caused.

As we arrived at the petting zoo, we were introduced to our new friends. One big fat kune kune boar, one big old turkey gobbler, one extremely stroppy and old emu and one very large and stinky undesexed goat.

Well, it all started rather sadly. The emu was in quite the state; his buddies had been rounded up and taken away, and, left behind on his own, he was clearly anxious. Knowing he would be too much for me and my inexperienced team we called in the local SPCA inspectors for help. One rounded the emu quietly from one direction and another inspector from the other. But the moment they had their arms around the emu's neck, his old and stressed heart literally stopped. I flew into vet nurse mode and administered mouth to beak and vigorously massaged his heart, but he was gone. My workers were completely at a loss. They had excitedly sat on the paddock's edge expecting to see an exhilarating rodeo act, but instead they got to see a majestic bird die literally of a broken heart. So far this was not turning out to be a fun mission.

The gobbler was an easy catch and we settled him into his crate relatively quickly. Then there was the boar that the team had already named Elvis. He fussed and grunted but we eventually guided him gently up the ramp to his side of the float. It was rewarding to see my young helpers breathe and take their time with him. They were learning that when it comes to animals, slow and steady wins the race.

So we had a turkey in the front of the float and a boar to the left of the back divider. We just needed a big old stinky goat to the right and we would be home free.

I had never seen horns quite as impressive at such close range. And boy, what a smell. Although the team were well briefed on remaining as professional and well-mannered as possible while we were out and about, I couldn't blame them for the choking and coughing, and even rolling on the ground, when the stench of the male goat hit our nostrils. He was an overpowering musky, toxic mess. And to top it off, to the kids' mixed delight and horror, he had demonstrated a nasty habit of cocking his leg, twisting his head around and weeing into his own mouth.

On the drive back to HUHA we all stank, and we could even taste the thick odour in the air of our double-cab ute as we drove with all the windows right down.

The very next day the workers were present as the vet neutered both Elvis and the goat they had fondly named Colonel Stinky. Desexing seemed to fascinate the team, appealing to some deep-seated macabre interest they held. Who knew castrating adult animals was such a thrilling business? But the transition to becoming testosterone-free was worth every drop of blood lost by these two seasoned gentlemen—with anaesthetics and pain relief they breezed through the messy and life-changing surgery. They were now socially acceptable and carefree. So after a mandatory stand-down period while all evidence of sperm left their bodies, the team helped me merge them in with their new four-legged families—there would be no more solitary confinement for these boys.

For Elvis, his new life meant lazy days lying in the sun, spooning his new kune kune friends. His only worry was what time breakfast would arrive on the back of the quad bike. He was as happy as a pig in mud and with the beautiful natural springs that threaded like veins through his paddock bursting from the ground, he literally was.

For the Colonel it was romance. He had caught the eye of Munchkin, a very sweet little goat that I had hand-raised after her mother had been shot by a hunter. She had been found alone in the bush and brought to us. Munchkin was a permanent resident at the sanctuary and her cheeky antics meant that she enjoyed hanging with the Community Maxers and often involved herself in their daily chores; she actually appreciated the company of her human friends more than that of other goats. So it was surprising and exciting when Munchkin became completely smitten with a non-human; she idolised Stinky and he her. The two of them ate, slept and adventured the deer-fenced paddock together, but their favourite spot on the property was a large purpose-built climbing frame, topped with a platform that had a view fit for a king and queen . . . and at HUHA Kaitoke that's just what they were.

CHAPTER 33

Stanley

Once again I found myself meeting a precious package in a carpark.

One of my friends had spotted an ad for a little dog on the Trade Me website. Apparently he was disabled and only had half a heart. I couldn't even begin to wrap my head around what that meant but said to my friend that if the family needed our help then we would be happy to step in. So little Stanley was put on the Petbus, a pet transportation service, and I was ready and waiting for his delivery.

'Oh my goodness!' My eyes widened as little Stanley was passed out the door and into my arms. I was totally enchanted. But I couldn't believe that anyone would have popped an animal this fragile on a bus to who knows where. Of course we weren't who knows where, but how did they truly know that? This little man needed some serious protecting and I vowed there and then to find out exactly what had happened to his crippled little body and to provide him with everything and anything he needed to keep him safe, happy and well.

The local vets puzzled at Stanley. They weren't too sure what was going on with his twisted limbs. So together Stanley and I journeyed up north to New Zealand's largest veterinary teaching hospital, where they had all the diagnostic bells and whistles at their disposal. I wanted some answers.

Oh, it was just too sad. The vets rattled off a list of things that seemed to be affecting Stanley's wee body: dwarfism, an overshot jaw, a tumour under his tongue, deformed little legs. All these ailments were most likely caused by a condition called storage disease, a rare inherited metabolic disorder.

I already knew a little bit about storage disease because years earlier a litter of huntaway pups had ended up on our doorstep. That night they were all over the news as these particular pups had been stolen from a research facility. They were tracked down to us and we were told by the police to return them. We hadn't been involved in their acquisition, but did feel strongly that we should see the situation they came from for ourselves.

So we had driven to Palmerston North and handed them back to their owner. Apparently the bitch was a private dog who was born with the disease. The researchers would borrow her so they could impregnate her with the sperm of another dog that carried the storage disease gene in the hope that their pups would also be burdened with the disease. We were told at the time that everything would be done to make sure that the pups' lives were as normal and wonderful as possible. What they didn't tell us was that the pups would only be grown to a certain age and then they would be killed and dissected in the name of science and improving medicines for people.

It was such a huge can of worms, and we were new to all of it. But the police knew we had the pups and we had to hand them back to the owner. It was heartbreaking but there was nothing else we could do.

And just a few years later here was Stanley with the same disease, except it wasn't—his was a rarer type. Stanley's version of the disease was closer to the one that human children got. He was a find of scientific significance. A month or so later the head of the research department in Palmerston North drove the five-hour round trip to see Stanley for himself and take some blood to confirm the find. He then set about pitching his plan to me.

They would like Stanley's sperm so they could impregnate one of the bitches who carried the gene. They were hoping that the pups would get Stanley's version of the disease.

'But won't you just kill the pups to dissect them?' I asked the researcher.

He looked me straight in the eye and in a honourably honest and frank manner said, 'Yes'. In an effort to seal the deal he continued, 'But we have underfloor heating in our kennels now, so they will be very comfortable and content before we have to kill them.'

'Hmm,' was all I could muster.

I listened to him telling me the long, complex stories of the children he had met with storage disease. He explained with great emotion and concern the suffering the children went through and how research on Stanley's pups could mean the difference between finding and not finding a possible cure or at least a way to prevent or understand the disease.

'Hmmm.'

I do care about people, of course I do, but it just wasn't right. I kindly declined his offer but, not wanting to be the reason for children suffering, I promised them Stanley's body when he died. I knew he would only be with us for a matter of months, so my promise was that I would let them know when the time was right and I would donate them his wee broken body. The decision sat right and as I explained the situation to the team their faces turned from horror to pride.

The Community Maxers had been amazing with Stanley. The admin team would sit him on their knees or up on their desks while they worked; the animal care team would take him in a little Paris Hilton-style carry bag and settle him down in the long grass while they picked up horse poo and did their chores. When we went on road trips Stanley came too. He was never alone and although his limbs could not carry him, the team did and he wanted for nothing. He was loved, cherished and pain-free. Until the tumour under his tongue grew just too large.

There were tears when I called the university research department, and when we walked in the doors to their clinic they treated us with nothing but respect. We cradled Stanley in our arms and showered him with tears of love as he shut his eyes for the last time. We were given a moment to say goodbye before they took his body away. Because Stanley had a rare version of the disease, his remains were flown straight to America to another facility where they would start work on him immediately.

Back at the sanctuary we had a debrief, and the team talked proudly about Stanley. They knew this little man, who they had treasured, protected, carried with them everywhere, while only small in stature, was possibly going to make a huge contribution to the world.

And then it was time to say goodbye to the Community Max team. Even years after they left us to go and conquer the world, Jim and I still can't help but smile fondly when we recall them. We ended up running the programme for twelve months before the government cut its funding, so all and all we had 24 young unemployed people come through the organisation and learn some 'HUHA magic', as we like to call it. In that time we even became the flagship charity for the Community Max Scheme and the kids were regularly interviewed on TV news and current affairs programmes. On several occasions I took them in to *Good Morning* to help me deliver a wonderfully informative segment.

While they were with us an extra grant had allowed us to upskill the workers. Some of them went on health and safety courses, some went on computer courses, all went on first-aid courses and those who still managed to hold a driver licence were sent off to wheels, tracks and roller courses, where they got an endorsement to drive tractors, diggers, forklifts and other machinery. It was so rewarding seeing their skills and CVs grow. By the end of their time with us eighteen of the 24 went on to become employed. Only two fell back into drugs, but I personally drove them to drug and alcohol counselling sessions while they were still with us, and I was proud to see them working hard at breaking the habit. One worker even went on to become a qualified vet nurse.

But the most rewarding part is knowing that each and every one of them now respects, values and understands animals . . . and each other. Now hopefully they also respect and understand authority figures, although every time Jim and I walk past the impressively well-constructed shelter that the building team laboured over for weeks we can't resist a smile. It is in fact a very fine piece of construction, which made us so proud of them, but we are also smiling because if you look very closely at the strange thick coat of bright pink paint inside the shelter, you'll see the reason why we made them paint it—to cover up the large penis they drew on the wall when they had finished building it, just because that's what teenagers do.

CHAPTER 34

The fine art of protest

My dad was one of those folk who had a highly tuned moral compass.

He could sniff out right from wrong a mile away and he was never afraid to voice his opinion—quite loudly, as I recall. My family probably saw it in me much earlier, but I first knew I had inherited his trait when I was working on a cruise ship as a cocktail waitress.

It was a complete con. 'Come sail with us, see the world and earn thousands of American dollars a month,' went their pitch. What they didn't tell you was that they would deduct from your wages thousands of American dollars a month so you would eventually end up trapped and in debt.

They had it down to a fine art. The three weeks training in Miami was amazing and all paid for—well, that's what we were told. But when we got there they said, 'Don't worry, we will just deduct the cost of the hotel from your pay.' Then there were the mandatory medicals, AIDS test, uniforms, flights to meet the cruise ship in New York—all deducted from our pay. Once on the ship our meals were provided, but we had to hire Colombian cleaners to clean our cabins and barbacks to wash the dishes in our bars; we had to pay them or they wouldn't be paid at all and of course it was deducted from our wages . . . it just went on and on.

We worked all hours and were then trapped on the bottom deck with some very inappropriately touchy feely Colombian men who only spoke Spanish. So to keep safe we would shut ourselves in. Every night I would drift off to the sound of the other girls crying. Most of them were from little villages in Europe and had come to America to find their fortune and to make their families proud. But as they slipped further and further into debt, the crying got louder and that's when my moral compass kicked in. I did try to talk to the officers first to find a solution, but it seemed that this was a racket that had been running for many years and they relied on a defeated workforce to run their ships. So I rallied the girls and told them that their families loved them and would hate to see them so distressed, that no American dream was worth what was essentially being held to ransom. Then I staged a walkout. When we returned from Bermuda we downed tools and walked out and refused to do anything more. The walkout didn't make the cruise company change its policies, but it gave us the immense satisfaction of taking a stand.

I heard from many of the girls over the following months; they were home safe and grateful and happy and stronger for the experience. And, like me, they would not be so gullible next time.

Jim, who is my sounding board, is not all that different to me in his genetic make-up in the stroppy disposition department. He, too, gets it from his father, Black Jock McKenzie. Jock was a boilermaker's union rep in the 1970s and had been responsible for the controversial stopwork on Wellington's Bank of New Zealand high rise, over the employer refusing to issue proper work boots.

So where this is leading is that from time to time, I would come across a situation that I just couldn't walk away from without a fuss.

Being on Facebook had certainly helped us grow in so many ways. We had direct access to the community and New Zealanders could follow our journey and see our work, and we could use it to voice concern over an issue. More recently HUHA has used Facebook to create New Zealand's largest nationwide march, which pressured the government into a law change on testing legal highs on animals.

Our first attempt at putting our toe in the water of controversy was just a small outburst back in 2011, but the public's reaction was quite the eye-opener.

My post went like this:

Grrrr. Yesterday I threw a wobbly in a Wellington store called Cranfields on the corner of Johnston Street and Lambton Quay. It's not my usual style but I was horrified to see their wide range of South African animal pelts proudly displayed as upper-class home decor. The zebra rug, eyelids, ears and nostrils included, cost $5320. So distressing. Join me in boycotting this money-driven heartless store!!

Maybe it was a bit over the top, but I had done a little research when I was in the store and had taken note of the company that supplied the pelts: Landed Gear. They were a South African business and not only did they farm the zebra and springbok pelts that I saw in the Wellington store, they also raised and killed giraffe. Yip, for several thousand dollars you could be walking over a giraffe skin rug in your bare feet while you boiled the kettle for your morning cup of char. Being a vegan, I get that a zebra or a giraffe is actually no different than a cow, but my theory was that the value attached to those pelts, as well as the eyelashes, ears and nostrils, made them designer trophy rugs, and in my book that's just wrong on so many levels.

So I emailed the store a message:

Hi, I passed my contact details on to your staff member yesterday. I would like to meet with you to discuss the African animal hides for sale in your store. During discussions with your staff member yesterday, she made it clear that your view is that everyone has the right of choice. She also said she did not believe that Wellingtonians would find the zebra hides offensive as they are sustainably sourced. I am writing to assure you that Wellingtonians do find these hides offensive to the point that a protest is being organised to take place in front of your store. I would encourage you to meet with me as this situation could easily be diffused if the hides were to be returned to the supplier. I do not want to give Cranfields a bad reputation as in many ways it is a lovely store. But in doing business with Landed Gear you have crossed a moral line.

Well, between the post and the email I managed to touch a nerve and with it came some good and some bad. The good was that the store was engaging, the bad news was that I naively didn't realise how much anger I was stirring up on Facebook.

Folk like me were having a knee-jerk reaction to zebras being dangled from shop fixtures and they set about writing some pretty hateful things. They called the shop assistants murderers and all sorts of other unsavoury names. I was starting to feel a little uneasy. I completely stood by my reasons for making a fuss but it's so important to communicate with manners, and to remain classy at all times. So I asked the

Facebook followers to please voice their views politely and with non-abusive consideration. But welcome to the world of social media; just because you start something does not mean you have any modicum of control. And for the very unhappy store owner it was quite an unpleasant ride.

They replied to my letter, saying they were shocked by some of the emails they had been receiving and included a quote from the Landed Gear website:

> *All of our hides are from sustainable sources. These include domestic farms or over population control programs. None of the animals that we supply are endangered or protected and as such comply with all domestic and international laws including the Convention on the International Trade of Endangered Species (CITES).*

They then asked me to supply some facts to back up my accusations, and to not contact the store staff as they had no say in what stock was carried. They finished by telling me they were a small family business, whose energies were currently tied up in a 'sad Christchurch situation'.

My response went like this (abridged):

> *Thank you for your response to my letter of concern.*
>
> *I apologise if you have been receiving 'shocking' emails. I can assure you that although others have mirrored my concerns, I am not aware of any individuals who would send abusive correspondence.*
>
> *I am also sorry you have been affected by the sad Christchurch situation. I took some supplies and volunteers down to assist and we returned with 47 unwanted animals. During my time in Christchurch I was overwhelmed by how positive the locals are.*
>
> *My reason for contacting you was initially fuelled after*

seeing a 'trophy' pelt hanging in your store. Although your staff member assured me that the hides were merely leftovers from legal sustainable farming, my view is that they are expensive objects of desire satisfying the dated and offensive trophy pelt market.

If these hides are merely fashionable leftovers and not trophy items then I am confused as to why they would be displayed with eyelids, nostrils and manes. I also wonder why the zebra hide is sold in your store at $5320, and the springbok hide only $250 ... this would reinforce my argument that zebra in particular is considered and sold as a trophy item.

Whatever the reason or excuse Landed Gear gives for the animals' deaths, it is not kind or couth. Incidentally, the giraffe hide also available from your supplier is worth approx $10,000 NZ. I can't even begin to imagine the sort of person who would invest in such tasteless cruelty.

I have travelled in South Africa and seen its government in action—I guess it is at your discretion as to whether you take solace in their farming practices. Having said that, whale meat is legal in some countries, bears dance in some countries and cat and dog is legally eaten in some countries— it just comes down to where you draw the line and I think you will find that Wellingtonians draw the line at importing upmarket home decor items/hides that are priced and look horrifically like trophy pelts!!

Please contact me if you have any further questions. I would like to be able to put this matter to rest in an amicable way.

In the end, Cranfields didn't want to meet up but they did stop stocking the skins. They told us they couldn't return or dispose of the pelts they did have because their business couldn't take any more financial hits.

I wrote a final post on the subject on Facebook.

The letters I wrote Cranfields were always professional and polite, but they forwarded me some of yours—jeepers I was shocked!!! Nevertheless thank you so much for all your wonderful commitment and support, WELL DONE WELLINGTON, I guess you could call that a win—a small win but definitely a win!!!

So I guess we had won. Because of our open and honest communication, we hadn't needed to protest, but it wasn't a feel-good victory and we had no real sense of closure.

It was also my first eye-opener into social media taking an idea and running with it. It is so important to always stay professional and polite and that is entrenched in all of our HUHA team, our work and our values. The work we do is so emotional and it would be easy to lose our temper or hurl abuse as a default reaction to the ignorance and cruelty we deal with daily. And yet we firmly believe that strategic and well thought-out interactions far outweigh any kind of mad ranting. We just wish sometimes our followers would understand our strategy and take a moment to breathe before reacting.

The early days at our old house on top of the hill, with Murphy and Haggis.

Ex-circus monkey Rachel was larger than life, but so gentle when meeting new friends.

Our team worked tirelessly during the Christchurch earthquakes to bring animals to safety. (© Jo Moore Photography)

Charlie and me relaxing in a paddock, with Captain Bungeye the cat. (© Jo Moore Photography)

Charlie loves iceblocks on a hot day.

It gets pretty cold at HUHA Kaitoke but with good shelter and food in their tummies the animals take it in their stride.

Three-legged Ned hitches a ride on the quad and helps feed out.

Henry the heron patrols his pond.

Winter magic at HUHA Kaitoke with Hugo, Tucker and Norm.

Ex-circus monkey Laurie would pass us his chain if he wanted to go for a walk.

Laurie gets such joy from painting, he even painted his house.
(© Jo Moore Photography)

Piggy Sue enjoys her freedom.

Some of the fantastic giant pumpkins that were grown in the community, shown off here by Cecil the duckling and his family of baby bunnies.

We had no idea she was pregnant: Pixie and newborn Punga.

Precious Stanley who touched so many lives when he was alive and went on to help save lives after his death.

Releasing one of the 300 fairy prions we rehabilitated after a devastating storm beached an estimated 250,000 birds on the North Island's West Coast.
(© Jack Penman)

CHAPTER 35

Saving nature from itself

'They are all dead and dying, Jim,' I sobbed down the phone. 'They are all dead and dying!'

Poor Jim. It was clear from my voice that I was semi-hysterical. I knew there was nothing he could do from the other end of the phone, but I just needed to tell him. With tears flowing and my nose streaming I felt weak and defeated. It was the most helpless and out of control I had ever felt in my whole career. I even contemplated throwing myself on the ground like an overwhelmed toddler . . . how devastating, how absolutely devastating.

The severity of the situation had hit the moment the beach came into view. I turned to Cherie, a volunteer at HUHA, and we looked at each other in sheer disbelief. Before us, in the foamy water's edge, lay hundreds of chubby little fairy prions, most of them dead and the rest of them dying. It looked like a massacre.

'Just get a grip and pick up the ones you can. Have you spoken to the zoo yet?' These were Jim's sage words of advice.

And so Cherie and I set to it, sifting through the endless dead for those still breathing.

A freak storm from the southwest was to blame for tens of thousands of fairy prions being blown off course and washing up on the beach, exhausted. The carnage reached way up the west coast of the lower North Island.

Our first stop was the Kapiti SPCA. They had been inundated with the survivors that the kind locals, who were out combing the beaches, had brought in to be cared for. The zoo was overloaded too and set about giving us all instructions so we could deliver the best possible chances of living to the highest volume of birds. Cherie and I stacked more birds into our car and said our goodbyes and good lucks to the small shelter. Although we had taken a huge load from them we knew it would be only a matter of hours before their little hospital was overburdened once again.

On the drive back to Kaitoke we were silent, maybe an unconscious effort to reserve our energy for the huge amount of work that lay ahead.

Jim came out to help us unload the 300 birds. He had made a hospital wing in our spare room. Wall to wall and ceiling to floor, dog crates had been stacked up and lined with towels and blankets and there were two large heaters warming the space. On the way home Cherie and I had stopped at a fishmongers and bought kilos of salmon. The team at the zoo had recommended we feed the birds around 15 millilitres of salmon slurry up to three times a day.

As the birds were settled in the cages and the blender began the first round in an endless procession of moulied salmon slurry, volunteers started to walk in the door. We had called ahead and rounded up the troops. We knew the task in front of us would be endless and for several days it was. Each bird was fed the fishy slosh through a tube into its crop, and one by one we worked our way through the birds. By the time we got to the last bird it was time to bring bird number one back out and start again. The mortality rate was huge. We lost about a third, who slipped into unconsciousness and could not be rallied. Cherie, Vari and Taylor and the rest of the volunteers were amazing with the desperate and tireless work, and we all stank beyond description.

On the first evening the team of vollies gave Jim, the kids and me a break. They all moved from the kitchen table to the spare room for an hour or so, so my funny family could pretend we were normal while we sang happy birthday to Jim and drank tea and ate cake. Everything tasted of fish but Jim was a trouper and understood that we were fighting for the lives of these special little characters.

Several days later we were testing the surviving birds' waterproofing by swimming them in a tub of sea water for long periods of time. Then we got a call from another bird rescuer who had organised the lifeguard to take us out on a boat to release the ones that were waterproof, fit and ready to face the elements again.

As the boat settled in the bay of an island off the shore of the Kapiti Coast, we set about opening the dozens of boxes and allowing the birds to gently float away. Once again I relished the amazing feeling you get when you set a wild animal free; it gives you such a sense of achievement and closure. A few of the wee birds struggled in the waves, so we scooped them up in nets, popped them into the boxes and took them back home for further care. The tricky thing with wildlife is timing: they really need to be released as soon as possible so secondary complications that come from being held captive do not arise, but then they need to be well enough to cope with the big wide world.

Usually it's people getting in the way of nature, but for this rescue it was Mother Nature who dealt the blow and people who came to the rescue. The communities of people scouring the beaches and bringing these special birds to safety can all be proud of themselves.

CHAPTER 36

A sad end

Jim was working inside the monkey enclosure, out of sight, when he heard some men talking in the trees behind our boundary fence.

'That's the one there, check him out.'

Jim thought nothing of it, and it wasn't until we saw Colonel Stinky strung dead from a pole in a hunting competition that we understood who the men were talking about that day.

Every Sunday for years, Jim and I have routinely driven to the fruit and vege markets in Wellington and loaded up on all the leftover produce of the day. The outing is quite fun, and we've been doing it for so long that we know everyone and they know us. We'd even managed to do a trade with the market manager, our ute for his old 6-tonne curtainside truck.

So as usual, one Labour Weekend Sunday, we were gone from our property for four hours. When we returned home, we set about feeding out our loot and that's when we noticed that Colonel Stinky was missing.

'I don't understand,' said Jim, scratching his head. 'He can't have gotten out from behind the deer fencing. And he would never leave Munchkin.'

But he was most definitely gone. So we set about scouring the hills and gullies, calling him. Stinky had become a firm favourite. He was a lovable character, especially since his hormones had settled after being neutered, and so surprisingly gentle even with the world's longest horns. In fact, now he could have been aptly named Colonel Cuddly. Munchkin, his dear friend, searched with us. She was beside herself and all we could do was talk to her and be there for her. But we were starting to feel very sick about the situation.

As the night settled and it became too dark to look we went back to the house for dinner and bed. It was about 2 a.m. when I shot bolt upright in bed.

'The hunting competition . . . was that this weekend?'

Jim turned the light on and sat up next to me. We were silent; there was no need to discuss what had happened to the ever-so-handsome Colonel. At that moment it all suddenly made perfect and horrific sense.

We were numb for the next day or so. We knew in our hearts what had happened, but we hadn't really processed how we would go about proving it. And then I remembered our friend Skin—Jane the pig's owner. I was sure he was one of the organisers of the hunting competition. When he picked up the phone I began to tell him our fears.

'So did anyone shoot a large white goat with horns that spread about 1.5 metres?'

He barely paused before saying he was pretty darn sure someone had, and the goat had won first prize for the best horns of the day. I asked him who entered the goat and he confirmed it was the scary neighbour's grandson.

'I'll get the photos in and run you off a copy,' he kindly offered.

I felt sick.

A few days later the photos arrived and there, hanging upside down from a rack, slit from chest to groin and gutted, was our big handsome man. Words couldn't begin to describe our grief as the reality of the situation sunk in.

Jim and I went outside and sat on our front doorstep with Munchkin who was, despite all the other gorgeous goats on the property, seeking human company again. We were in shock.

I talk to my family a lot. We are close and often run things past each other so as I was relaying our shock and distress to my eldest brother Stephen he simply said, 'Hey, do you want me to tell the guys at work? They may be able to tell your story.' Stephen is a news cameraman.

Soon after the police left, the TV news arrived, then the newspapers and finally, to make the situation even worse, the parasites of reality television came sniffing around. We had a call from the producers of *Neighbours at War*, who tried to sweet talk me into doing their show. I laughed and said no thanks; I thought it was really trashy TV.

As the weeks passed by the *Neighbours at War* folk really started to get nasty. They told me that our scary neighbours were prepared to be on the show and if we didn't appear then they would show us in a poor light. And that's just what they did.

Cherie and I saw the *Neighbours at War* film crew prowling our fence line, settling on a muddy spot where the cows had stood during the winter and puckered up the grass turning it into mud. We hid inside the house and peeked from behind the curtains. It was clear from the angle of the shot that they were going to present the muddy corner as the general condition of our property. Cherie was a rock as I paced up and down, reeling from the stress of feeling victimised and violated. She snuck out the front door and took some pictures of the crew that summed up the whole programme. I felt reprieved as

I looked at the screen of the camera. The photo showed the crew filming a tight shot of the neighbours standing and pointing at a muddy paddock but from the elevated position the truth was clear. The mud they were passing off as our standard was just a corner of the paddock and in the wide photo you could see it was surrounded by acres of lush green grass and beautiful valleys full of native plants. *Neighbours at War* and my neighbours were the perfect match.

Months later as we sat and watched the show when it aired for the first time, we felt sick all over again. I had tried everything I could think of to cancel the show, and I had told the producers repeatedly that they were siding with the man who stole and killed our goat and lied to the police. But as we sat through what we believed to be drivel and lies about how the scary neighbours had been so wrongly accused and how awful it was to live by us, there was a surprising twist at the end. The voiceover announced that after further investigation the police had found that the neighbour had in fact stolen and killed our goat. Well, what a complete waste of time and stress that was.

The sad thing was that the TV show just added fuel to our neighbour's fire. We had won again and so they lashed out by starting a HUHA Haters page on Facebook for everyone to see.

Despite their efforts HUHA likers seem to grow at a rate of 100 likers to one hater. It's funny because although it should be all about the likers, it's always the one negative comment that gets under our skin. It is really frustrating that these hater folk seem to be allowed to just make things up. The things they say about us are just absurd. But in situations like this, Taylor Swift is right: it's best just to shake it off.

We've learnt to follow the advice 'Don't engage with the

nutters'. In the past if we ever tried to defend ourselves or pacify these types of people it always made things worse, or it made us look defensive. And the other advice we take is 'Don't poke the bear'. Sometimes it is very hard to resist doing this when we have a sneaky peek at the comments made by our serial haters on social media. Gosh, it can be hard to read so much rubbish and just sit on our hands, but engaging with the nutters or poking the bear just heightens the drama and creates an audience. It gives them our time and our consideration, two things that they just do not deserve. We are better off directing our attention to rescuing animals. And so we just ignore them as more and more twisted lies about us or photos of skinny animals that we have never met appear on social media. We politely smile, keep our chins up and focus on what is important—the animals that are in our care.

CHAPTER 37

In the nude

Through the thick sea of animal rescues, at-risk youth and neighbourhood drama, we realised that we needed to be smart about being sustainable.

I had started a small business with a friend called Stephanie, with the aim of securing a future for her kids and mine and for Jim and HUHA. Our plan was to grow an ethical skincare business, one that, like HUHA, walked the walk. The first product I presented to Steph was an animal healing balm. I'd been using it for years and having carefully extracted compounds from many of the herbs myself I knew what it was capable of. But together we decided to turn our attention to people products.

The brief we gave ourselves was to develop a skin care range that was scientifically proven to work while being cruelty free, natural and vegan—oh, and we would work towards palm-oil free products too. Both parties put in capital to pay for branding and product development, which meant another mortgage commitment from Jim and me. But we knew we had the talent, the drive and the skill to make something big happen.

It took just a few days to come up with the name: Nude Natural Skin Care. Although that is quite a popular name nowadays, back then we were the first and naively we thought we would be the only. We did manage to register a trademark for Nude in New Zealand, but were advised that because nude was a descriptive colour in skin care the offshore trademark authorities would not grant us protection. But undaunted we plunged on developing our brand presence and started to get it into the shops.

Stephanie has a saying: 'You don't know what you don't know', and what we didn't know was that we were about to enter the world of quite an unexpected and unbelievable bout of what felt like industrial sabotage. We tell this story today with a sense of humour, first because we survived and second because it was just so bizarre.

One day when Googling our name—as you do—we stumbled across a website-holding page. A new product line called Nude Skincare was about to be launched in the UK. Thinking that that wouldn't do, we gave them a friendly heads up that we already existed and fully intended to sell in the UK market and that thanks to our trademark they would never be allowed to sell in New Zealand. We assumed that the matter would be over and hoped they'd learn to do their research before encroaching on someone else's brand.

And that's when things got interesting. Steph started getting calls from England and Europe at 2 a.m., people asking where they could buy our Nude Natural Skin Care. Then Steph's wheelie bin was stolen. Her home address had been listed with the Companies Office and as far as anyone was aware it was the HQ for Nude. There were several other strange events that all happened at the same time, and when we checked in with our trademark attorney, he smiled and said, 'Oh, that's pretty standard; they haven't done anything to you that any of us in this business wouldn't do.' He explained further that this other

Nude skin care company was just fact-collecting and it would seem that they were getting ready to fight us. Our brand, our investment and our futures were under attack and we wanted to know who these people were.

They had alluded in a reply to our letter that they were worth millions and we had better get out of their way. Their Nude products had now landed in New Zealand and were visible as full shop window advertising, and it was revealed who owned the company that had become our Goliath. It was Ali Hewson, the wife of Bono from U2. So the letter had been right—their client was worth millions.

Did I mention that the UK business turned things around and said that because they were bigger and could have a stronger brand presence then they would look into suing us if we didn't go away? After getting over the shock of having invested our hard-earned money in a brand we could only sell on our own website or to friends and family, we turned a corner and took our business in another direction. (We do still sell Nude Natural Skin Care on our website . . . it just seemed wrong to cave in to bullying.)

I was fixated on the idea of using a New Zealand native resin in a product we were developing; it had amazing antimicrobial properties and recent research had proven its healing benefits. The problem was that the resin would not break down in aqueous products—products that could dissolve in water—which would limit its use. I spoke to the supplier and he told me that he did have a water-soluble version but that it was formulated using petrochemicals. He said if there was a way to break the resin down naturally he'd be rich and that a scientist at the industrial research labs had been working on it for the past five years.

Well, that was it. Game on. I may not be a scientist, but I am the sort of person who never says never. There had to be a way and, thanks to my grandfather Bill, I had inherited the most oddly inventive mind. It didn't take long to ponder a solution; in fact it was back in the shower as I was conditioning my hair that I was struck by an idea. I rushed to our lab and set about formulating. My solution was easy, it was cost effective and it worked. I sent a sample to the resin supplier who said my invention was significant and a game changer.

Stephanie set about patenting the idea and I was soon enlisted to problem-solve for other companies. We had renamed our company Innate, 'instinctively natural', and as the weeks turned into months it was apparent that we were now in the business of being formulators of natural ingredients. If anyone was told that a certain type of natural product was not possible, then we were the go-to place to prove it was. From health products to environmentally friendly bilge-pump cleaners, we could do it. Even the top manufacturing plants in the country called upon our services. Maybe it's because I'm not a scientist that I can see things differently. But whatever it was, it worked. And with Steph's organisational skills we were confident we would go far.

The only thing was we were still in a lot of debt and unable to pay ourselves. But we were building the future and we knew that one day our pay day would come; we just had to work hard and be patient. So at nights I continued to work on Innate projects in my funny little lab and rescue and rehabilitate during the day. And Jim continued to support all my efforts, putting all his trust in the fact that one day the pressure would lift.

I was and am determined that HUHA should be a voluntary-led charity. I love the idea that workers are with us due to passion, not for a pay cheque. I have seen before the complacency a 9 to 5 attitude brings to a shelter. My ultimate dream is to one day be able to award food vouchers to volunteers; I want to support those who support HUHA, but I want it to be smart support. So I hold fast to the idea that by making Innate a success, then I can infuse some of that success into HUHA. And as the years pass we are getting closer to that goal. Through innovation and thinking outside the square (I'm referring to both Innate and HUHA) we will make the biggest change!

CHAPTER 38

Christchurch

If there is one thing that Facebook has taught us it's that New Zealand is a village.

Through this site we can all access each other at the touch of a keyboard, no matter where we are. And we are all connected by our pride for our country and our people.

When the news came through that Christchurch had been rocked by a second and deathly earthquake, New Zealand was in shock. I distinctly remember pacing up and down anxiously; it was such a hopeless feeling knowing that there was nothing we could do. And then I wondered if maybe that wasn't true.

I called all the big animal agencies to see what I could do to help but they thanked me and said they were leaving things to the experts to deal with. I rang my friends at the SPCA Rescue Unit and asked them what they needed. Soft collapsible cat cages was their response. So I rang around until I found a company willing to donate some. Next I looked at the social media pages to see if I could find something else to help with. I read about 50 horses cut off from a water supply just out of Christchurch, whose owners were distressed and didn't know what to do. So I called them and asked them if I could help. I then called around rural and farm supply stores and found a large tank that just might be a solution. I organised a truck to deliver it and spoke to a woman about getting a tanker of water to be delivered. It was surprisingly easy as everyone I spoke to was feeling like me; they just wanted to help.

And this is how I did it, as reported in *The Dominion Post*, a Wellington newspaper:

WELLINGTON WOMAN'S HORSE MERCY MISSION

A Wellington woman has arranged for a tanker to deliver much-needed water to 50 thirsty horses in Heathcote today.

The horses at the Heathcote Valley Riding School were in desperate need of water in 'forgotten' Heathcote Valley, resident Kathryn Byfield said.

'A lot of people have been talking about Lyttelton and Redcliffs and Sumner, but Heathcote has been forgotten,' she said. 'We've lost everything—the coffee shop, pub, the dairy.'

Today, Byfield said a woman from Wellington had heard her call for help and had arranged for a 5000 litre tanker from Ashburton to deliver water to the horses.

'Thank you so much,' she said.

Bridle Path Road was still cordoned off, with workers removing loose rocks from the area, but they would 'find a way' to get the water right to the horses.

Byfield, who owns three of the horses, stayed in her damaged Heathcote home for two nights, before staying with relatives in Brooklands and Riccarton.

'I've basically had my life in my car,' she said.

Water was turned back on at her house on Monday, but was still not available at the riding school.

Power had been restored, but portaloos had not been delivered to the suburb. 'It's a waiting game,' she said.

Volunteers, many of whom have been displaced from their homes, had been carting water to the horses every day.

Twenty horses, belonging to individuals, had been transported to other areas, but it was too difficult to move the 50 belonging to the riding school, she said.

'How do you ship out 50 horses? I don't know when things are going to come back on.'

Moving the horses was a concern, with many roads 'stuffed', and some horses too young to put in floats.

However, with the arrival of the water tanker the horses would not need to be moved from their home, she said.

It was great to help, but it didn't feel like enough. I called some friends in Christchurch to get their take on things. The problem was that when the quake hit all of the shelters were already full, and there was nowhere to put the hundreds of lost and displaced animals. I called Jim.

'Hey, what if we took our truck to Christchurch to help?' I said, crystallising my thoughts. 'We could bring back shelter animals and that would leave a place for lost animals to wait safely until they were reunited with their owners.'

'Yip, let's do it,' said Jim without a second's pause.

So we set about planning the most effective trip we could. Sam worked at Kiwi Rail and organised us free passage on the ferry. I sent Cherie down first in our people mover to scout things out and help where she could while I organised pallets of food and cat litter from local suppliers who were happy to help. The organisation that had accepted our help first was a cat rescue. They were overwhelmed and extremely grateful for any support. We drove through the night in the truck and as the sun rose in the sky we saw firsthand the complete devastation and reality of what had transpired. As we made deliveries and picked up animals, the ground kept shaking.

Back on the ferry we had 47 cats, plus turtles and roosters along with three dogs we picked up from a great charity called Dogwatch. We were exhausted but happy we had relieved even the tiniest bit of pressure. An amazing team of volunteers back in Wellington were ready and waiting. They had organised a cattery to take the cats while we set about rehoming them and the roosters and turtles came back with us to HUHA.

And then another strong quake hit the city just a few months later in June 2011. Christchurch was in crisis again and we flew into action to plan another trip, in fact two more trips.

The Interislander allowed us free passage again, and this time our destination was Dogwatch. They were drowning in dogs and desperate for our help. Last time we had taken only three of their charges because we were unknown to them. But by now we had formed a relationship with them and we were their biggest hope. We had done a shout-out on Facebook asking for North Island people to come forward and offer to rehome or foster a Christchurch dog, and the response had been incredible. Vari, Cherie and I were on the road for days, visiting families and doing property assessments. It may have been a national disaster, and time was of the essence, but it was still so important that we knew every home that every dog was going into. We needed to set up all families and dogs to succeed, otherwise the mission would be pointless. These animals needed safety and security, and they needed it fast.

So with volunteers taking calls and coordinating possible homes and us property checking, we felt like we had everything covered.

On the two trips down south and back we managed to rehome another 50 dogs in just two weeks, 44 into permanent homes and six into foster homes. As the truck landed in Wellington, a very tired Jim and I, along with Vari and Taylor, who had taken a second car and helped execute the mammoth rescue, parked up at Wellington Animal Control. We pulled back the curtain sides of the truck so that the preapproved families could be introduced to their very scared and tired new family members.

Most of the match-making was spot on, though as expected a few families struggled and the dogs had to be relocated to other families that were a better match. But all in all it was an amazing success. We remember each and every one of the animals we relocated from Christchurch, and we have promised Dogwatch, the new families and the dogs themselves that we will be there for them for the rest of their lives should they need us.

Once a HUHA animal, always a HUHA animal.

CHAPTER 39

Doing what we do well

A few months earlier I had been voted on to the board of the Wellington SPCA.

It was a bit of an honour as I was to sit alongside some pretty prestigious people. Though the greatest honour was the faith that the general public was starting to have in me. I had recently won a Local Hero award through Kiwibank's New Zealander of the Year awards, and now, as the ballots were counted, I was the people's top pick to help turn the SPCA around.

I had finally crawled out of the shadows and could now stop apologising for causing a fuss. People wanted me to cause a fuss; they wanted me to be their voice and steer the animal welfare ship onto a healthier and more productive path. The good thing about schmoozing with the bigwigs is that you can get real insight into what makes a place tick, and for the SPCA at that moment I felt anything could be possible.

At this point both the Wellington SPCA staff and the public were made aware of the major and relentless financial strain the organisation was suffering, so it was clear they needed to take a different tack if they had any hope of forging a sustainable future and surviving. But the now business-savvy Wellington SPCA was starting to implement new, tougher policies in an attempt to dispel the perception that they were at the public's beck and call as a dumping ground and a source of free or cheap veterinary services. That sort of attitude was sucking the important age-old institution dry. So out of necessity came the time of the 'managed entry' policy. While I understood the motives behind this policy and other similar changes, I struggled to come to terms with the impact it had on the animals. If someone fronted up with an unwanted animal, whether their reasons were right or wrong, and they were turned away . . . what happened to the animal, where did it end up, what was its fate? To me, rejecting an animal because of a policy was just too simplistic and, sadly, stories that I felt gave my concerns credence started to trickle in.

One day a woman named Sue called me on my HUHA phone. She had only just learned of HUHA from a friend and she desperately wanted our help and advice. Sue had befriended a homeless man living it hard on the streets of Wellington. Every few days she would check on this man, named Dave, bringing him blankets, clothes and food. Slowly but surely she had formed a simple but comforting friendship with him and during that time he learned that he could trust her. Sue had approached the Salvation Army, who already knew of the man, and explained that she was determined to help. Together Sue and the compassionate Army staff began working on an intervention plan, with their aim being to get Dave safely off the streets and into a rehabilitation programme.

There was just one four-legged problem—a little Jack Russell called Syd. Syd was Dave's constant companion; the two were inseparable. They had spent many a night huddled together, cold and hungry. While the streets had been home to both of them for more than a year, living so desperately rough had also taken a tragic toll. Dave and Syd's situation was a deathly serious one and Sue knew she was their only hope.

When Dave was approached with the plan for him to leave the streets, he was understandably full of mixed emotions. Mostly he was very reluctant to let Syd go. But as Sue gently encouraged him and explained that the separation would ultimately save both their lives and that they would each have a fresh start and a promising future, Dave gingerly conceded. Syd would have the life the wee dog deserved. So after a few false starts the three of them drove sombrely to the Wellington SPCA.

When they arrived and Sue explained their predicament and asked to sign Syd over to the organisation, the receptionist shook her head and told them that unfortunately they couldn't just walk in the door and leave him there. She suggested that they go to the pound.

Sue couldn't believe what she was hearing; she had worked so hard to gain Dave's trust and she had told him that he could also trust the SPCA and that Syd would be in loving, kind hands. As she pleaded in a very dignified way for the receptionist to reconsider she could feel her perfectly coordinated plan start to unravel. Dave was already on a knife's edge, it really would not take a lot for him to spook and return to the cold hard streets. The receptionist insisted that the pound was their only option, apologised and said goodbye.

As they drove to the pound Sue and Dave were fearful and overwhelmed with emotion. Sue internalised her worry because she had heard how harsh pounds could be. As her mind raced, she questioned herself and rechecked her motives but kept a positive façade for the very wobbly and teary Dave. This was a nightmare.

The very next day on the phone to me, Sue was composed but I could hear the anguish in her voice. She had left Syd at the pound with a very nice lady just the day before and she was now panicking that she may have made a mistake and that if anything untoward happened to Syd she would never forgive herself. She asked me if there was anything that HUHA could do to help to assure Syd's safety. I asked her which pound it was and when she said 'Wellington' I sighed in relief—Syd was with Vicky. I knew instantly he was in safe and capable hands.

I made a quick call to Vicky and she confirmed that Syd was in her care—she had even taken the funny little character home with her the previous night. I smiled to myself; Syd had enjoyed his first soft bed and warm and toasty home in over a year. Vicky was confident that she would find him just the right forever home. When I told Sue she cried tears of complete relief.

Sue went on to complain about her experience with the Wellington SPCA and in fact I queried it too. It was such a sensitive situation; surely Syd should not have been turned away in such a finite manner, surely some problem-solving would have led to a solution or at least a compromise or modicum of hope? The point I made to the shelter CEO was that this, in my view, was an example of why each scenario needs to be assessed at face value, case by case. It is my belief that a blanket approach shouldn't be applied in any life-and-death situation, no matter how many scenarios an organisation is faced with every day—each case is different and each case deserves full consideration. Dig deeper and try harder seemed to be my go-to catchphrase for quite some time . . . in fact it probably still is today!

As the weeks went on, I heard of more animals being rejected and some even euthanised for reasons I could not fathom. I understood, probably more than most, how overwhelming society's demands could be on a charity. And I agreed with the strong emphasis the Wellington SPCA was placing on education—the community needed to clean up its act and take responsibility. But when those within the community could not help, when there was no one to vouch for an animal, it was so important for shelters to open their doors and their minds, engage and to problem-solve.

In contrast—and with hope—I thought back to a day when I was called by an SPCA shelter manager who had been struggling with salmonella in the cattery and was going to have to euthanise all of the cats in their main room not yet rehomed, as that had been the protocol for any serious disease outbreak in the shelter for years. I was in my car and on the way as soon as I hung up the phone.

Shaun had moved out and we now had a spare room. These cats didn't need to die, they just needed quarantining until they tested clear for the bacteria. So nine cats came to live in our spare room and, with the help of caring HUHA volunteers and SPCA staff, all nine cats went on to new and loving homes. That was the sort of problem-solving that could be achieved if we all pitched in together. That is the can-do attitude we need to strive for every day.

But I realised that my voice was not as strong as the business-first attitude that, in my view, was placing a stranglehold on the passion, determination and creative thinking that was needed to save every single animal's life—or at least have a darn good crack at it. Then I remembered an important lesson my wise mum had taught me:

'Don't worry about what others are doing, just do what you do well.'

And there it was, the solution was right there in front of me—I could reinvest my energy into HUHA and open another shelter. We needed to pick up where help and support had dropped off.

I was proud of our achievements at HUHA Kaitoke, and

I was beginning to understand just how different we were. With that all-important knack for thinking outside the square and problem-solving that we had so passionately developed, we had already achieved so much. But we were still predominately a farm animal sanctuary and I was beginning to see that Phase Two needed to be about companion animals.

I lasted three years on the board of the SPCA but in the end I knew that I personally could help the animals more by growing HUHA. We needed to walk all that talk, we needed to lead by example.

Every day I would receive dozens of phone calls. More and more people were hearing about our work and more and more people were either wanting to help out or get involved in some way. It was so lovely to see the HUHA magic catch on. My theory was working; the more I said the word 'we' instead of 'me' the more the community realised that HUHA wanted them to step in and get involved.

One day I got a message that stood out.

Hi HUHA, my name is Claire Thornton, I've worked at a vet clinic and even travelled to Thailand to rescue dogs as part of a tsunami relief team. I am a mum of three and I very much want to be involved with HUHA.

I instantly smiled. It wasn't what this Claire Thornton said; it was the stubborn determination I could hear in her voice. She sounded like just our cup of tea. Claire was up the Kapiti Coast so I referred her on to Sam to help with a pending chook rescue. That would be a great starting point, I thought, and I carried on washing the dishes and quietly pondering to myself.

CHAPTER 40

HUHA magic

Who would have thought a book fair could change so many lives?

We had managed to borrow a vacant store on State Highway 1 in the small coastal town of Waikanae. Sam's good friend and others had donated boxes and boxes of books for us to sell to raise some much-needed funds. As we set up the trestle tables and unpacked the boxes, people started to trickle through the door. I scanned the room, watching folk browse through hundreds of books. I listened to them chat among themselves.

'Yes, it's such a wonderful organisation.'

'Oh, I've been following them for years, what an inspiration they are.'

'I work full-time and can't keep animals myself, but I do my bit by sharing them on Facebook.'

'I have a HUHA dog.'

'I have a HUHA cat.'

'My aunty has a HUHA pig.'

The stories were endless, and as people were keenly hunting

out book bargains they seemed just as intent on sharing their HUHA connections. I was completely proud. I felt like a mum sitting on a park bench at a playground, watching my child making new friends.

One lady approached me and told me all about HUHA. She told me how it began and all about the Christchurch rescues and that the founder Carolyn, who she had met once, was a regular on *Good Morning* TV. I listened to her story as she spoke with such assurance and passion. I didn't have the heart to correct any of the details or to tell her that it was me she was talking about. I just took it all in and marvelled that we had managed to affect so many lives. We weren't just growing in numbers, we were growing compassion through the strength of our message. It seemed to be giving folk hope and pride and all the good feelings that people need in life.

My attention turned from the customers to the volunteers. There were only half a dozen but they were working the room with gusto, and one in particular stood out. I hadn't met her before but instantly recognised her voice.

'Hi, you must be Claire?' I introduced myself, and continued, 'Sam said you've been helping with the Kapiti chook runs, thank you so much.'

As we started to natter there was an instant connection. I knew immediately. This was the woman who was going to help me build HUHA into a force to be reckoned with.

Following the success of the book fair there was an article in the local newspaper elaborating on what HUHA was and that we were looking for land in Kapiti to start a second shelter.

I had been meeting with Claire and some other wonderful volunteers to look at different properties for sale. Aside from a very kind offer of a deposit loan, we didn't really know how we were going to pull it off. We just knew that once we found the right location that we would find a way. As we wandered around the various lifestyle blocks Claire and I made plans.

'Who's going to run the new shelter?' asked a volunteer.

'I will,' chirped Claire without a moment's hesitation.

And that's just what happened.

A week or so later we got a call from an elderly man who owned a dilapidated horse stud farm. He wanted to know if we would be interested in renting the stable block and 14 acres of land in the centre of his 110-acre property.

It was a dream come true and we signed on the dotted line just a few days later.

Here is what we posted on Facebook:

Yippee, we have some fantastic news. We have just secured our new Kapiti HUHA HQ site, and it couldn't be any more amazing!

We are so lucky; the property owners have agreed to let us lease the facilities while we get established, with a view to buying it a little further down the track.

We take possession next week and can't wait to have you up for a visit.

The purpose of the new Kapiti HUHA HQ is to have a facility that welcomes visitors, volunteers and supporters, provides an educational outlet and of course is safe and nurturing for all animals.

Our new facility is located in Otaki at an old stud farm and we are quickly converting some of the 42 stables into safe and comfortable kennels, chicken runs and wildlife rehab aviaries. We think the administration block will be ideal as a cattery. And the paddocks and yards will facilitate our equine assisted therapy and educational lessons. We also hope to develop medicinal herb gardens.

We had agreed to pay $2500 per month for the old building and paddocks. For me it was much more than a lease; it was an insight into whether we could handle a mortgage as somewhere in the not-so-distant future our plan was to own our own property, one we could purpose-build into a safe and practical haven. In the meantime we would work with what we had and not miss a single payment until our bank saw that we were a good risk and capable of anything. (A sneaky peak three years into the future, with not a payment missed, will show that's just what transpired.)

So we started to scrub and clean the tired old building, fix the plumbing and electrics, and build fences. Sam and her new enthusiastic team of volunteers focused on the horse paddocks and yards, which had been built with non-treated and now rotting timber, and Claire and I rallied a team to turn the stables into a dog sanctuary. Each of the concrete block stables in this once grand old building that even boasted a clock tower were three metres square—plenty of room for beds and couches so that the unwanted dogs coming into our care had a soft, warm place to rest their bones. For some it was the first time they had ever felt comfort. For others it appeased the pain of finding themselves homeless.

Who knew that the dilapidated stables would soon become New Zealand's leading no-kill animal shelter? And that with our small committed group of volunteers we would change animal welfare outcomes and expectations so dramatically? We had no idea that our formula of time, patience and pure determination would save so many hundreds and thousands of animal lives. We were different and we were already proud.

We didn't have to bow to outside pressure because we were marching to the beat of our own drum. That's not to say we didn't have our challenges, but we've embraced and conquered every hurdle and we've done it with good old-fashioned common sense. Others soon joined us, such as

Sally who is our feisty Pom and has steadfastly made HUHA her life's work too.

My theory was that Kaitoke was to be our farm animal and wildlife base, as well as a home for the long-term oldies and wonkies. Because of the neighbours and the driveway dramas, I couldn't grow Kaitoke to meet the demands of the growing public interest, so it was settled that Kaitoke only be open by appointment on Sundays. This respected the privacy of the animals there in our care that often had extra special needs. Otaki would become the 'shopfront' of HUHA, open seven days a week to welcome visitors and volunteers. With all hands on deck, the Otaki shelter didn't just address the needs of the animals, it also provided exposure for dogs and horses available for adoption. It was a place where folk could walk, play and interact with the animals then apply to adopt if a connection was strong.

Soon the animals started to trickle in. The first dogs were two heavily pregnant bitches, Jodi and Poppy, whose puppies were too far along to be considered for termination. Jodi whelped at Sally's house and then raised her scrumptious puppies at the shelter surrounded by love, comfort and our incredibly doting team. When Poppy struggled with her newborn pups, Jodi was able to relieve the burden by taking two on as her own; the problem-solving was already working.

Sam found herself busily responding to a cry for help. There was a large herd of unhandled Kaimanawa and Kaimanawa-cross mares, foals and an assortment of yearlings that were being sent to slaughter after their owner had become ill. Sam set about organising the rescue; we would need to pay the equivalent price of the meat for each life and then transport them from the back blocks of Ruatoria to the safety of HUHA Otaki. It was the first time in all my years that I had handed over the reins on a big rescue and although I struggled and wobbled a bit from the sidelines like an anxious parent, I was so proud of Sam and her new team. They pulled off a miracle, transporting 21 of the horses with the support of Kaimanawa Heritage Horses to the safety of our care without a hitch. And our biggest asset was once again the power of Facebook, which we used to fundraise quickly and easily for the logistically mammoth task and to find many potential new homes for the horses.

Sam and her team then set about working with the wild herd, patiently gaining their trust and setting them up with the skills they would need for their new lives. As each left us, a contract was signed by the carefully vetted owners saying that they could not breed from, give away or on-sell their companions—if, for whatever reason, they could no longer care for the horse they were to come back to HUHA, so we could understand what happened and put it right. That is a condition that applies to all of our adoptions. We promise to take responsibility for all HUHA animals for the rest of their lives. No HUHA animal should ever end up passed around, lost in the system or on Trade Me.

Claire is an absolute legend. She hit the ground running as more and more dogs came into our care at the new Otaki shelter. She is so invested and passionate about every life in her charge. Once again I learnt it was okay to let go a little. I was abreast of every situation and at the forefront of every decision, teaching the team all I could from Jim's and my experiences, but with our new Otaki HUHA open every day, and me constantly dashing between the two shelters, I had to learn to sometimes steer the ship remotely and trust in Claire's instincts.

In the beginning we didn't want to step on the SPCA's toes, so we only took in the death-row dogs from the pound. But very quickly we realised that for many animals in New Zealand we were their only chance—they needed us, so we opened the floodgates and braced ourselves.

As animals arrived at both shelters our philosophy was simple: love and patience. We have no deadline on the animals' care, there is no race to get them out the door and no expectation for how quickly they will rehabilitate. And if they do not fit the mould we do not consider them failures. We just welcome them as family and enrich their lives to the best of our abilities. And through the love and time we offer up, we notice huge changes. One perfect example of this is Tinkerbell.

When I walked into the old farmhouse everything looked normal; the fire was warm and the children were snuggled in their onesies, the adult dogs seemed calm enough outside the window, but there was something amiss with the puppy we had been asked to collect. I knew she was deaf—that was the reason we had received the usual 'come and get this puppy or we'll shoot it' call—but she had such an edge about her for one so young. She was cute, incredibly cute, but there was definitely more going on with this beautiful white eight-week-old Staffy pup than what lay on the surface. As I went to scoop her up in my arms she flinched and growled. I blamed myself; she's deaf so maybe I hadn't given her enough of a visual warning.

I was saying my goodbyes, paperwork signed, when the dad stopped me. He had forgotten to show me their favourite game. He placed the deaf puppy on the floor, and as she settled on the mat the man crept up behind her with a broom clasped in his hands. I could hear the children start to giggle with delight as their dad shoved the broom at the puppy from behind. Getting an almighty fright she swung to action, teeth bared, snarling and growling in a frenzied effort to ward off the attacking broom. The puppy's eyes were wide and the growls continued as I picked her up, her heart racing as the family chortled and raved that the game was much more fun when she was asleep . . . she was getting better at fighting back too, apparently.

Sitting on my couch at home she relaxed and slept for hours on end, though if a person or a cat brushed past her she was up and ready to attack. With a new name and surrounded by love at HUHA's Otaki shelter, we hoped that Tinkerbell could start to forget her past.

Tinkerbell learnt to play nicely with other dogs and enjoyed all the attention she received from the volunteers. The mixed-up little girl was finally getting a stable and kind upbringing and her frenzied attacks, which always stemmed from a place of feeling threatened, lessened. We were careful not to let anyone play tug toy or initiate any games where she had to use her mouth, and she was always treated calmly and gently. Because Tinks was deaf she learnt to watch the people who cared for her and follow their lead. She learnt rules and boundaries and that the world was good and that she was welcome in it.

Other shelters had taught me that the only remedy for aggression in dogs was to euthanise. But HUHA was starting to have its own voice and philosophies. We wanted to know why animals acted the way they did and if it was possible to remedy learned behaviours. And so it was through Tinky and the passion of her number-one fan Claire that we discovered we had a very valuable commodity on our side: time. And with that time we reinforced our mantra that by changing the environment we could change the animal. We helped Tinky detox from her old life and taught her to trust again. We didn't enable her fear by mollycoddling; we just simply taught her through routine and boundaries to trust people and respect all other beings. And the recipe worked.

When Tinkerbell was ten months old a wonderful lady called Tracey came into the shelter and on seeing Tinky showed an interest in adopting her. We told Tracey about Tinkerbell's history and asked her to visit for a few weeks so she could get a true understanding of the gorgeous character Tinky had become. Tracey and her son diligently showed up for walks and play dates. They started to learn sign language and the rest is history. They adopted Tinkerbell who now has her first real home. The three of them are often seen around their home town, Tracey and son on their bikes and Stinky Tinky on her lead, pulling the way.

As you will have realised by reading about my journey, Tinkerbell wasn't the first to challenge all that I had been taught about responsible decision-making in an animal shelter. But she was the first real challenge for our new HUHA team, reinforcing that digging deeper, trying harder and taking the time to problem-solve pays off.

This little white deaf dog was the beginning of our journey to becoming New Zealand's first truly no-kill animal shelters. We didn't label ourselves no kill and then strive to meet the challenge. For us it just happened organically; we are no kill because it is what it is. People often ask me what no kill means and this is what I tell them: we value the gift of euthanasia for old or infirm animals, when the time is right. To hold them in your arms and to say goodbye surrounding them with love and dignity is a sad but beautiful thing. But we do not euthanise for man-made reasons: for time, money, ignorance, space or convenience. At HUHA every animal is valued beyond words, and every animal is given the right to a sensible, safe and bright future.

We think that maybe, just maybe, we have set a new bar. With our HUHANZ Facebook community and our team we're on track to change animal welfare expectations and outcomes in New Zealand—so watch this space.

Or, better still, join us on this magical but achievable journey of hope.

Epilogue

From here on it is all about keeping these promises:

- To the animals: we won't give up on you. We will be patient while you learn and grow, and we will be considerate as we find you the right happy ever after.
- To the team: we will always support each other and welcome newbies as we grow. We will never allow pressure or others to dictate our decisions.
- To HUHA: I will not stop until we find a way to build a sustainable future for this special charity.
- To the community: we will always keep you involved, as it is ultimately you who can make the biggest change.
- To myself and Jim: I will never forget where we started or why. And that we will learn from our mistakes along the way.

Acknowledgements

I want to say a huge thank you to the special people who have laughed, cried and had penny-dropping moments with me along the way.

Starting of course with my truly wonderfully normal but inspiring family and ending with my wonderfully driven and slightly abnormal HUHA family.

You all mean the world to me and it is your constant conversation and patience around my vision and passion that has allowed me to be bold enough to walk such a unique and important path.

I'd especially like to mention Eric who steadfastly encouraged Jim and me to realise our potential for the sake of the animals.

And to Donna Lee my teacher who inspired me to heal.

About the author

Carolyn Press-McKenzie is well known as the founder of HUHA Helping You Help Animals Charitable Trust. Carolyn's inspired problem-solving and drive has led a team of HUHA volunteers to save thousands of animals from death row and to find safe outcomes for hundreds of animals after the Christchurch earthquakes, thirty beagles from a medical testing facility, thousands of hens from battery farms as well as ex-circus and zoo animals and native wildlife. HUHA volunteers also organised New Zealand's largest animal welfare protest—against party-pill testing on animals—after which the law was changed.

Carolyn currently heads HUHA's two no-kill animal sanctuaries just north of Wellington as well as running a business that formulates natural products. She has worked as a vet nurse, trained animals for film and television, studied herbalism, appeared as the animal adviser on TV One's *Good Morning*, has won two New Zealander of the Year Local Hero Awards and is highly regarded by the animal lover community.

For more information, visit www.huha.org.nz